TABE TEST 11 & 12 READING AND LANGUAGE ARTS STUDY GUIDE: PRACTICE QUESTIONS FOR PREPARATION FOR THE READING AND LANGUAGE EXAMS (LEVELS E, M, D, AND A)

The TABE Test is a trademark of Data Recognition Corporation, which is not affiliated with nor endorses this publication.

TABE Test 11 and 12 Reading and Language Arts Study Guide: Practice Questions for Preparation for the Reading and Language Exams (Levels E, M, D, A)

© COPYRIGHT 2007-2020 Exam SAM Study Aids & Media.

All rights reserved. No part of this publication may be reproduced, stored in a retrieval system, or transmitted, in any form or by any means, electronic, mechanical, photocopying, recording, or otherwise, without the prior written permission of the copyright owner.

ISBN: 978-1-949282-61-0

NOTE: The TABE Test is a trademark of Data Recognition Corporation, which is not affiliated with nor endorses this publication.

TABLE OF CONTENTS

Test of Adult Education TABE 11 and 12 Format	1

READING SKILLS SECTION

Reading Practice Set 1 (40 questions Levels E – D)	3
Reading Practice Set 2 (40 questions Levels M – D)	16
Reading Practice Set 3 (40 questions Levels M – A)	27
Reading Practice Set 4 (40 questions Level A)	38

ENGLISH LANGUAGE SKILLS SECTION

Grammar Guide

Adverb Placement	51
Commonly-Confused Words	51
Misplaced Modifiers	52
Parallel Structure (Parallelism)	52
Pronoun-Antecedent Agreement	53
Pronoun Usage – Correct Use of *Its* and *It's*	53
Pronoun Usage – Demonstrative Pronouns	54
Pronoun Usage – Relative Pronouns	54
Proper Nouns and Proper Adjectives – Capitalization	55
Punctuation – Using the Apostrophe for Possessive Forms	55
Punctuation – Using Colons and Semicolons	55
Punctuation – Using Commas with Dates and Locations	55
Punctuation – Using Commas for Items in a Series	56
Punctuation and Independent Clauses – Avoiding Run-On Sentences	56
Restrictive and Non-restrictive Modifiers	56
Sentence Fragments	57
Subject-Verb Agreement	57
Subordination	58
Review of Verb Tenses	58

Source, Reference, and Citation Guide	59

Grammar and Usage Exercises

Grammar and Usage Exercises – Set 1 (15 questions Levels E – M)	61
Grammar and Usage Exercises – Set 2 (15 questions Levels E – M)	62

Grammar and Usage Exercises – Set 3 (15 questions Levels E – D)	64
Grammar and Usage Exercises – Set 4 (20 questions Levels E – D)	66
Grammar and Usage Exercises – Set 5 (20 questions Levels E – D)	68
Sentence Formation and Essay Development Exercises with Tips (25 questions Levels E – A)	71
Punctuation and Capitalization Review Exercises (20 questions Level M)	80
Sentence Correction and Revision Exercises	
Sentence Correction and Revision Practice Set 1 (10 questions Level D)	84
Sentence Correction and Revision Practice Set 2 (10 questions Level D)	85
Sentence Correction and Revision Practice Set 3 (30 questions Levels D – A)	86
Sentence Correction and Revision Practice Set 4 (30 questions Levels D – A)	89
Combining Sentences and Identifying Fragments (25 questions Levels D – A)	93
Identifying Correctly-Written Words and Sentences (20 questions Levels M – A)	98
Word Meaning, Relationships, and Context (15 questions Level A)	102
Citation and Referencing (5 questions Levels M – A)	104
Writing Skills Exercises (25 questions Levels M – A)	105

Answers and Explanations:

Reading Practice Tests	112
Grammar and Usage Exercises	125
Sentence Formation and Essay Development	129
Punctuation and Capitalization Exercises	131
Sentence Correction and Revision	132
Combining Sentences and Identifying Fragments	137
Identifying Correctly-Written Words and Sentences	139
Word Meaning, Relationships, and Context	140
Citation and Referencing	142
Writing Skills	142

Test of Adult Basic Education (TABE) Format

The Test of Adult Basic Education 11 & 12 evaluates the achievement of students in the core academic areas that are assessed as part of Adult Basic Education programs. The TABE is also used to assess high school equivalency.

The Test of Adult Basic Education 11 & 12 has three subtests:
- Reading
- Language
- Mathematics

Each section of the test will usually have 40 scored questions.

This publication is devoted to reading and English language skills.

Reading Skills:

You will be tested on the following reading skills on the TABE Test:

- Understanding main ideas and specific details in a text
- Interpreting the author's tone, style, claims, strategies, and purposes
- Drawing inferences and conclusions or making predictions from a text
- Determining the meanings of words and phrases in a text
- Analyzing other aspects of texts, such as organization, structure, and word choice

The reading practice questions in this publication cover all of the skills mentioned above.

The texts in the TABE 11 & 12 reading subtest will be mainly on informational, scientific, and historical topics. There may also be some literary texts.

Accordingly, there are informational, scientific, historical, and literary texts in the reading skills section of this book.

English Language Skills:

The language part of the exam covers all of the following aspects of the English language, which are included in the "English Language Skills" section of this study guide:

- Grammar, usage, sentence structure, and paragraph development
- Relationships between words and word meanings
- Spelling, capitalization, and punctuation
- Editing and correcting a written text
- Understanding various text types and purposes

Question types:

The questions on the TABE will be of the following levels of difficulty

- E – Easy
- M – Medium
- D – Difficult
- A – Advanced

The questions in each part of this study guide have been labeled to indicate their level of difficulty.

TABE 11 & 12 Math

You may wish to see our other publication for the math part of the test:

TABE 11 & 12 Math Practice Tests: 250 TABE 11 & 12 Math Questions with Step-by-Step Solutions

Reading Skills Section

READING PRACTICE TEST 1

Instructions: Read each article and answer the questions following it. When you have finished, you can view the answers and explanations at the back of the study guide.

SPECIAL INSTRUCTIONS FOR INTERNATIONAL ORDERS

Four large rectangular containers have been placed by the rear door of the shipping room. We have placed a special staging station in the middle of the room. The special staging station is for international orders.

All of the packages to be shipped internationally will be placed in the staging area. This will be done by the packaging department. Each package must be placed into the appropriate container as follows:

- Container A is for packages that weigh 16 ounces or less.

- Container B for packages with a weight of over 16 ounces, up to 32 ounces.

- Container C is for packages that weigh more than 32 ounces but less than 80 ounces.

- Container D is for all packages that are 80 ounces or more in weight.

- Container E is for all packages that have been damaged. These will be sent back to the packaging department. This will cause the order to be delayed by 2 days.

If the packages are not sorted correctly, they will be rejected for shipping. In this case, the customer's order will be delayed more than five days. This will very negatively affect our online customer ratings. We cannot afford for this to happen.

1. What could cause an order to be delayed more than two days? **(E)**
    A. A package is not sorted correctly by its shape.
    B. An 80-ounce package is placed in Container D.
    C. A 16-ounce damaged package is placed in Container E.
    D. A 32-ounce damaged package is placed in Container B.

2. In which container should an item weighing 80 ounces be placed? **(E)**
    A. Container C
    B. Container D
    C. Container E
    D. Containers C or D

3. Where is the staging area located? **(E)**
    A. By the rear door
    B. By the four large rectangular containers
    C. In the middle of the room
    D. By the packaging department

Go on to the next page.

Baking a cake is easy. But you need a good oven and the correct ingredients. You should first of all pre-heat the oven to 350 degrees. The correct temperature makes your cake moist and fluffy. So, be sure that the oven is pre-heated correctly.

Next, grease and flour your cake pan. Then mix your ingredients together. Mix the dry ingredients together. Then add the wet ingredients.

Your dry ingredients are one and a half cups of sugar, one teaspoon of salt, two teaspoons of baking soda, and two cups of sifted flour. Check that your bowl is big enough before you put anything in it.

Then mix the dry ingredients well in your bowl. Now add one-half cups of vegetable shortening, two eggs, one cup of whole milk, and a teaspoon of vanilla.

Put the mixture into the cake pan. Then bake for 30 minutes, and enjoy!

4. Based on the instructions, failing to pre-heat the oven could result in: **(E)**
   A. the cake being burned.
   B. the cake taking longer to bake.
   C. insufficient time to prepare the cake pan.
   D. the cake being dry and heavy.

5. What should one do after preparing the cake pan? **(E)**
   A. add the wet ingredients
   B. check that the mixing bowl is large enough
   C. mix the sugar, salt, baking soda, and flour together
   D. add the shortening, eggs, milk, and vanilla

[1] The world's first public railway was very modern and useful. The train could carry passengers. But it was mainly designed to transport coal from inland mines to ports. These ports were located on the North Sea. Its first journey was on September 27, 1825.

[2] The train had thirty-two open wagons. It could also carry three hundred people. The locomotive steam engine was powered by the steam-blast technique. The steam traveled into the engine via a narrow pipe. In this way, the steam created a huge draft of air. The air created more power and speed for the engine.

[3] The train had rimmed wheels which ran on top of rails that were specially designed. These rails gave the carriages a faster and smoother ride. The locomotive could accelerate to fifteen miles per hour. This was a record-breaking speed at that time. However, the carriages were very small.

[4] The inventor of the locomotive was George Stephenson. He later improved his steam engine by adding twenty-four more pipes. The engine then had twenty-five tubes instead of one. So, Stephenson's second train was even faster and more powerful than his first one.

Public Railway Facts	
1) First Journey	September 27, 1825
2) Number of Wagons	32
3) Number of Passengers	300
4) Number of Pipes on First Train	1
5) Speed of Travel	15
6) Number of Pipes on Improved Train	25

6. According to the article, why was the second train better than the first one? **(E)**
   A. It was more spacious and comfortable.
   B. It could carry more passengers.
   C. It contained more pipes and tubes.
   D. It was faster and had more power.

7. **Part A**
   What is the main idea of the article? **(E)**
   A. Stephenson's train ran quickly and comfortably.
   B. The first train was specially designed.
   C. The first train was an important and practical invention.
   D. The engine of the first train was quite small.

8. **Part B**
   Which two sentences support the answer to Part A? **(E)**
   A. The train could carry passengers.
   B. But it was mainly designed to transport coal from inland mines to ports.
   C. These ports were located on the North Sea.
   D. Its first journey was on September 27, 1825.
   E. The train had thirty-two open wagons.
   F. The air created more power and speed for the engine.

9. Which row of the chart most clearly supports the information in paragraph 4? **(E)**
   A. 3
   B. 4
   C. 5
   D. 6

Go on to the next page.

[1] Jean Piaget is one of the most well-known theorists in child development and educational psychology, and the scholastic community still discusses his principles today. Focusing his research on the processes by which human beings learn how to exist in their environments, Piaget strived to answer the question: "How do human beings obtain knowledge?" He is responsible for discovering what he termed "**abstract symbolic reasoning**." This term refers to the notion that biology impacts upon child development much more than socialization. Piaget determined that younger children responded to research questions differently than older children. His conclusion was that different responses occurred not because younger children were less intelligent, but because they were at a lower level of biological development.

[2] As a biologist, Piaget had an intense curiosity in the manner in which organisms adapted to their environments, and this interest resulted in several revolutionary theories. Piaget postulated that children's behaviors were regulated by mental structures called "schemes," which enable a child to interpret the world and respond appropriately to new situations. Piaget observed the process by which human beings have to learn how use their mental structures as they become familiarized with their environments, and he coined the term "equilibration" to describe this process.

[3] The biologist noted that all children are born with the drive to adapt, and he therefore posited that mental schemes of adaptation are innate. While an animal continues to use its in-born adaptation schemes throughout its entire existence, human beings, in Piaget's view, have innate schemes that compete with and then diverge from constructed schemes, which are those that are acquired as one interacts with and adapts to his or her social environment.

[4] The process of adaptation, which is split into the two distinct functions of assimilation and accommodation, was of paramount importance in Piaget's research. The function of assimilation refers to the way in which a person transforms the environment in order to utilize innate cognitive schemes and structures. Alternatively, the term accommodation is used to describe the way in which pre-existing schemes or mental structures are altered in the process of accepting the conditions of one's environment. For example, the schemes used in bottle feeding or breast feeding a baby illustrate the process of assimilation because the child utilizes his or her innate ability to for suckle to carry out both tasks. Further, when a child begins to eat with a spoon rather than a bottle, he or she uses accommodation since a completely new way of eating must be learned.

[5] As Piaget's body of research expanded, he identified four developmental stages of cognition in children. In the first stage, which he called the sensorimotor stage, Piaget observed that at the **incipience** of the child's cognitive development, intelligence is demonstrated in the manner in which the infant interacts physically with the world. In other words, intelligence is directly related to mobility and motor activity at this stage. In addition, children start to obtain language skills and memory, which Piaget termed "object permanence," in this initial developmental stage.

[6] As a toddler, the child begins the pre-operational stage, which is quite egocentric. So, most of his or her intellectual and emotional energy is self-centered rather than empathetic at this point of development. Although intelligence, language, and memory continue developing during this time, thinking is mainly inflexible and illogical.

[7] The concrete operational stage begins at approximately age five. Logical and systematic thought processes appear during this stage, and the child begins to comprehend measurement and symbols pertaining to concrete objects, such as numbers, amounts, volumes, lengths, and weights. The egocentrism of the previous stage begins to diminish during the concrete operational stage as thinking becomes more logical.

[8] The final stage, termed the formal operational stage, begins at the start of the teenage years. This stage is normally characterized by abstract thought on a wide range of complex ideas and theories. However, research has indicated that adults in many countries have not completed this stage due to the lack of educational opportunities or poverty.

10. **Part A**
    Which of these describes the author's main purpose? **(M)**
    A. To provide biographical information about Jean Piaget
    B. To discuss the significant aspects of Jean Piaget's theories on child development
    C. To criticize the research of Jean Piaget
    D. To point out flaws in current child development theory

11. **Part B**
    Which two sentences from the article best supports the answer to Part A? **(M)**
    A. As a biologist, Piaget had an intense curiosity in the manner in which organisms adapted to their environments, and this interest resulted in several revolutionary theories.
    B. Piaget postulated that children's behaviors were regulated by mental structures called "schemes," which enable a child to interpret the world and respond appropriately to new situations.
    C. As Piaget's body of research expanded, he identified four developmental stages of cognition in children.
    D. Piaget observed that at the incipience of the child's cognitive development, intelligence is demonstrated in the manner in which the infant interacts physically with the world.
    E. The final stage, termed the formal operational stage, begins at the start of the teenage years.
    F. The concrete operational stage begins at approximately age five.

12. Based upon paragraph 1, which is the best explanation for the term abstract symbolic reasoning? **(M)**
    A. Older children are more intelligent than younger children.
    B. Older children are more physically developed that younger children.
    C. Older children are more socially developed than younger children.
    D. The intellectual development of children is affected by their biological development.

13. According to paragraph 2, the following statements about Piaget are true except: **(M)**
    A. Piaget's work as a biologist had a profound impact upon his research on child development.
    B. Piaget understood that mental development is closely connected to biological development.
    C. Piaget realized that biological factors affected child development, in addition to environmental factors.
    D. Piaget was the very first researcher on the subject of child development.

14. Which word means the same thing as "incipience" in paragraph 5? **(M)**
    A. start
    B. prime
    C. mental
    D. active

15. Why does the author mention bottle feeding in paragraph 4 of the article? **(M)**
    A. To identify one of the important features of assimilation
    B. To exemplify the assimilation process
    C. To describe the importance of assimilation
    D. To explain difficulties that children face during assimilation

16. According to the article, which of the following statements best characterizes the sensorimotor stage? **(M)**
    A. The growth of the child's intelligence in this stage depends predominantly on his or her verbal ability.

B. The skills obtained during this stage are of less importance than those achieved during later developmental stages.
C. During this stage, the child learns how his or her mobility relates to language.
D. The child's cognitive development in this stage is achieved through physical movement in his or her environment.

17. **Part A**
Based on the information in paragraphs 6 and 7, what does the author suggest about child development? **(D)**
A. Before the child enters the concrete operational stage, his or her thinking is largely rigid and unsystematic.
B. The conceptualization of symbols is not as important as the conceptualization of numbers.
C. The child becomes more egocentric during the concrete operational stage.
D. Memory and language become less important during the concrete operational stage.

18. **Part B**
Which detail from the article best supports the answer to Part A? **(D)**
A. As a toddler, the child begins the pre-operational stage, which is quite egocentric.
B. So, most of his or her intellectual and emotional energy is self-centered rather than empathetic at this point of development.
C. Although intelligence, language, and memory continue developing during this time, thinking is mainly inflexible and illogical.
D. The egocentrism of the previous stage begins to diminish during the concrete operational stage as thinking becomes more logical.

In December of 1880, a friend who was a veterinary surgeon gave Louis Pasteur two rabid dogs for research purposes. Victims of bites from rabid dogs normally showed no symptoms for three to twelve weeks. By then, however, the patient would be suffering from convulsions and delirium, and it would be too late to administer any remedy.

So-called treatments at that time consisted of burning the bitten area of skin with red-hot pokers or with carbolic acid. Pasteur devoted himself to discovering a more humane and effective method of treatment for the disease. His tests on the rabid dogs confirmed that rabies germs were isolated in the saliva and nervous systems of the animals.

After many weeks of tests and experiments, Pasteur cultivated a vaccine. Derived from a weakened form of the rabies virus itself, the vaccine is administered before the microorganism is encountered and stimulates the immune system to recognize and fight off any future exposure to the organism.

Just after Pasteur had treated his first rabies patients in France successfully, four boys from New Jersey were bitten by a dog that was believed to have been carrying rabies. The boys were sent to Pasteur for treatment. A national campaign was launched, which created a media sensation. It appeared that everyone in the States was following the progress of the four boys, who returned home from France as celebrities. They even went on a media tour.

In spite of the existence of the vaccine, rabies is still responsible for many deaths around the world each year. Incidents of rabies in humans are now very rare in the United States, however. This is because pets are usually vaccinated against the disease. In addition, the vaccine is widely available. However, this was not the case in the past. Many animals and humans suffered greatly from the disease before the vaccine was discovered.

19. Patients today would probably respond to the idea of treatments that were used in the past with: **(M)**
    A.   fear
    B.   bewilderment
    C.   scorn
    D.   apathy

20. The primary purpose of the article is to discuss: **(M)**
    A.   pasteurization and the rabies vaccine.
    B.   the life and work of Louis Pasteur.
    C.   Pasteur's discovery of the rabies vaccine.
    D.   experimental research on rabid dogs.

21. **Part A**
    The author implies that the discovery of the rabies vaccine was significant for which one of the following reasons? **(M)**
    A.   It prevented animals from suffering during scientific experiments.
    B.   It helped many people avoid physical suffering and death.
    C.   It caused the treatments for other diseases to become more humane and effective.
    D.   It contributed to the prevention of the contagion of germs, in general.

22. **Part B**
    Which detail from the passage best supports the answer to Part A? **(M)**
    A.   By then, however, the patient would be suffering from convulsions and delirium, and it would be too late to administer any remedy.
    B.   His tests on the rabid dogs confirmed that rabies germs were isolated in the saliva and nervous systems of the animals.
    C.   Just after Pasteur had treated his first rabies patients in France successfully, four boys from New Jersey were bitten by a dog that was believed to have been carrying rabies.
    D.   After many weeks of tests and experiments, Pasteur cultivated a vaccine.

23. Which of these timelines shows the correct function of the rabies vaccine? **(M)**

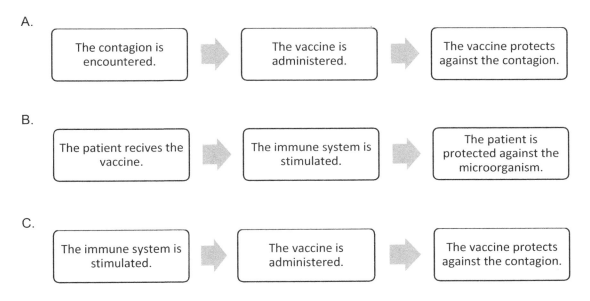

D.

| The microorganism is encountered | ➡ | The vaccine is administered. | ➡ | The immune system is stimulated. |

[1] The discipline of archeology has been developing since wealthy European men began to plunder relics from distant lands in the early nineteenth century. Initially considered an upper-class hobby, archeology in general and archeological field methods in particular have undergone many developments and experienced many challenges in recent years.

[2] Before the field excavation begins, a viable site must first be located. While this process can involve assiduous research, sometimes sheer luck or an archeologist's instinctive hunch also come into play. A logical locality to begin searching is one near sites in which artifacts have been found previously. Failing that, an archeologist must consider, at a minimum, whether the potential site would have been habitable for people in antiquity. Bearing in mind that modern conveniences and facilities like electricity and running water were not available in pre-historic times, the archeologist quickly discerns that sites near rivers and caves could provide the water and shelter indispensable for day-to-day living in such inhospitable conditions.

[3] Once the site has been located, the process of surveying commences. This means that the ground surface of the site is visually scrutinized to determine whether any artifacts are protruding through the soil. The archeologist then digs test pits, small holes that are equidistant to one another, to determine what the boundaries of the larger final pit will be. Once these dimensions are determined, the hole is dug and sectioned off with rope or plastic.

[4] The excavation, which is a meticulous and lengthy process, then begins in full. The archeologist must gauge the texture and color of the soil carefully as the pit becomes deeper and deeper since variations in soil composition can be used to identify climatic and other living conditions. It is imperative that the walls of the excavation are kept uniformly straight as the dig progresses so that **these differences** can be identified.

[5] The soil that is removed from the pit is sifted through a sieve or similar device, consisting of a screen that is suspended across a metal or wooden frame. After the soil is placed in the sieve, the archeologist gently **oscillates** the device. As the mechanism goes back and forth in this way, the soil falls to the ground below, while larger objects are caught in the screen.

[6] Throughout this process, all findings are entered in a written record to ensure that every artifact is cataloged. This activity can certainly be tedious; yet, it is one that is critical in order to account for each and every item properly. Each finding is placed in a plastic bag bearing a catalog number. Subsequent to this, a map of the excavation site is produced, on which the exact in-situ location of every artifact is indicated by level and position.

[7] Finally, the arduous task of interpreting the findings ensues. During the last two centuries, various approaches have been utilized in this respect. Throughout the early 1800's, most fossil recovery took place on the European continent, resulting in an extremely Euro-centric method of examination and dissemination of findings. Unfortunately, as a consequence, the misapprehension that the origins of homo-sapiens were European began to take shape both in the archeological and wider communities.

[8] Recent research suggests that inherent social and cultural biases pervaded the manner in which archeological findings were investigated and explicated during the early nineteenth century because little attention was paid to the roles that wealth, status, and nationality played in the interpretation of the

artifacts. These problems began to be surmounted, however, in the 1860's, with the advent of the theories of Charles Darwin on the origin of the human species.

[9] Darwinian theory, the notion that human beings are the ultimate product of a long biological evolutionary process, then infiltrated the discipline of archeology and heavily influenced the manner in which archeological artifacts were recovered and analyzed. By the middle of the 1900's, the imbalance created by the cultural biases began to be rectified as there was a surge in artifacts excavated from African and Asian localities.

24. The words "these differences" in this article refer to: **(M)**
    A. climatic conditions
    B. soil variations
    C. excavation walls
    D. dig progression

25. According to the article, what do archeologists consider when choosing a potential site for excavation? **(M)**
    A. whether research can be conducted on the site
    B. whether electricity is presently available
    C. whether the site existed in pre-historic times
    D. whether any data was previously collected from areas near the site

26. The word **oscillates** in this article is closest in meaning to: **(M)**
    A. inculcates
    B. exculpates
    C. manipulates
    D. vibrates

27. Why are artifacts recorded in a written catalog? **(M)**
    A. to ensure that no items are lost
    B. to prepare a map of the site
    C. to understand the item's in-situ location
    D. to prepare them for long-term storage in plastic containers

28. **Part A**
    Which of the following statements accurately expresses the author's attitude about the Euro-centric method mentioned in paragraph 7? **(M)**
    A. It was regrettable, but necessary.
    B. It was completely unavoidable.
    C. It was regrettable because it created cultural misunderstandings.
    D. It only took place within a small geographical area.

29. **Part B**
    Which detail from the passage best supports the answer to Part A? **(M)**
    A. During the last two centuries, various approaches have been utilized in this respect.
    B. Throughout the early 1800's, most fossil recovery took place on the European continent, resulting in an extremely Euro-centric method of examination and dissemination of findings.
    C. Unfortunately, as a consequence, the misapprehension that the origins of homo-sapiens were European began to take shape both in the archeological and wider communities.
    D. Recent research suggests that inherent social and cultural biases pervaded the manner in which archeological findings were investigated and explicated during the early nineteenth century

30. Based on the information contained in paragraph 9, what can be inferred about the early 1900s? **(M)**
    A. There were few archeological findings from Africa and Asia.
    B. Darwinian theory had little effect on archeology.
    C. All archeological findings were culturally imbalanced.
    D. Charles Darwin recovered many artifacts.

31. Which of these is the best summary of the article? **(M)**
    A. An archeologist has many things to consider when selecting a site. Protruding artifacts can create difficulties during the excavation. Most importantly, the European archeological discoveries of the 1800's should be disregarded.
    B. Protruding artifacts can create difficulties during the excavation. Preparing written archeological records can also be tedious. However, cultural prejudices should be avoided when archeological findings are being interpreted.
    C. An archeologist has many things to consider during site selection, excavation, and interpretation. The excavation of an archeological site must be a meticulous and methodical process. Finally, cultural prejudices should be avoided when archeological findings are being interpreted.
    D. The excavation of an archeological site is a meticulous and methodical process. Preparing written archeological records can also be tedious. Most importantly, the European archeological discoveries of the 1800's should be disregarded.

Two original forms of theater have emerged from Japanese culture: Noh and Kabuki. Noh, the older form, was originally established to meet the demands of the "discriminating Japanese aristocracy" and remained "unchanged for more than six centuries."

Noh renders mundane, everyday activities, like drinking tea or arranging flowers, into exquisite artistic performances. Consisting of minimal spectacle, bare stage designs, and little spoken dialogue, Noh is classified as more ritual than drama. In order to convey the dialogue, a chorus sings the protagonist's lines while the performer engages in the "solemn act" of the dance.

Kabuki performances are discernably different than those of Noh. Based on puppet theater, Kabuki is designed to meet the tastes of the general populace, rather than those of the aristocracy. According to long-standing theatrical custom, Kabuki performances can be extremely long, lasting up to twelve hours in some cases.

Since movement plays a greater role than dialogue, Kabuki actors must wear heavy makeup and engage in highly stylized actions. Because of its appeal to the general populace, Kabuki theater remains as fascinating and exotic as it has always been, even though its purity has been somewhat compromised through exposure to other cultures.

32. The use of quotations in the article suggests which of the following about followers of Noh? **(D)**
    A. They lament the fact that Noh clings on to outdated customs of the past.
    B. They want to emphasize that followers of Noh are traditional, discerning, and serious.
    C. They fear that the popularity of Kabuki theater may diminish the appeal of Noh.
    D. They plan to make Noh more up-to-date in order to increase its following.

33. The fourth paragraph implies that Japanese audiences today would respond to Kabuki theater with: **(M)**
    A. admiration
    B. impatience
    C. confusion
    D. boredom

34. Followers of Noh and followers of Kabuki would probably agree with which one of the following statements? **(M)**
    A. Theatrical productions sometimes last too long.
    B. Japanese theater is unlikely to change in the future.
    C. Theatrical performances should be highly stylized and full of spectacle in order to be effective.
    D. Japanese theater is an important and interesting aspect of Japanese culture.

[1] Equating the whole history of the struggle of humankind to that of the class struggle, the social and political writings of Karl Marx have been the impetus of a great deal of change within society. According to Marxism, the political school of thought based on Marx's doctrines, the working class should strive to defeat capitalism, since capitalistic societies inherently have within them a dynamic that results in the wealthy ruling classes oppressing the masses.

[2] The nation state is seen as an instrument of class rule because it supports private capital and suppresses the common person through economic mechanisms, such as the taxation of wages. Because growth of private capital is stimulated by earning profits and extracting surplus value in the production process, wages have to be kept low.

[3] Since capitalism reduces the purchasing power of workers to consume the goods that they produce, Marx emphasized that capitalism inheres in a central contradiction. Under the tenets of Marxism, capitalism is therefore inherently unstable.

[4] Marx asserted that productive power ideally should be in the hands of the general public, which would cause class differences to vanish. These idealistic writings have had a huge impact on culture and politics; yet, many believe that Marx's work lacked the practical details needed to bring about the changes to the class structure that he envisaged.

35. The primary purpose of the first two paragraphs is to: **(M)**
    A. discuss why the writings of Karl Marx have had such enduring social and political importance.
    B. explain the basic tenets of Marxism.
    C. discuss the consequences of private capital.
    D. critique the existing class structure and oppression of the masses.

36. Which of the following best describes the relationship between the four paragraphs in the article? **(D)**
    A. The first two paragraphs give an assertion, while paragraphs 3 and 4 refute that assertion with statistical evidence.
    B. The first two paragraphs explain a long-standing problem, and paragraphs 3 and 4 provide the potential solution.
    C. The first two paragraphs introduce and expound upon a theory, while paragraphs 3 and 4 point out criticisms of the theory.
    D. The first two paragraphs give the background to the topic in a general way, and paragraphs 3 and 4 provide specific details about the topic.

37. The writer mentions the "huge impact" that these writings have had on culture and politics in the last sentence in order to: **(D)**
    A. juxtapose this impact to Marx's failure to include pragmatic instructions in his work.
    B. highlight the way in which capitalism is often unstable.
    C. reiterate the importance of giving power back to the general populace.
    D. lament the social change that Marx himself predicted.

I cannot say that after this, for five years, any extraordinary thing happened to me, but I lived on in the same course, in the same posture and place.

For this purpose, that I might do everything with discretion and consideration, I fitted up a little mast in my boat, and made a sail too out of some of the pieces of the ship's sails which lay in store, and of which I had a great stock by me. Having fitted my mast and sail, and tried the boat, I found she would sail very well; then I made little lockers or boxes at each end of my boat, to put provisions, necessaries, ammunition, and so on into, to be kept dry, either from rain or the spray of the sea; and a little, long, hollow place I cut in the inside of the boat, where I could lay my gun, making a flap to hang down over it to keep it dry.

I fixed my umbrella also in the step at the stern, like a mast, to stand over my head, and keep the heat of the sun off me, like an awning; and thus I every now and then took a little voyage upon the sea, but never went far out, nor far from the little creek.

At last, being eager to view the circumference of my little kingdom, I resolved upon my cruise; and accordingly I victualed my ship for the voyage, putting in two dozen of loaves (cakes I should call them) of barley-bread, an earthen pot full of parched rice (a food I ate a good deal of), a little bottle of rum, half a goat, and powder and shot for killing more, and two large watch-coats, of those which, as I mentioned before, I had saved out of the seamen's chests; these I took, one to lie upon, and the other to cover me in the night.

It was the 6th of November, in the sixth year of my reign - or my captivity, which you please - that I set out on this voyage, and I found it much longer than I expected; having secured my boat, I took my gun and went on shore, climbing up a hill, which seemed to overlook that point where I saw the full extent of it, and resolved to venture. In my viewing the sea from that hill where I stood, I perceived a strong, and indeed a most furious current.

And now I saw how easy it was for the providence of God to make even the most miserable condition of mankind worse. Now I looked back upon my former abode as the most pleasant place in the world and all the happiness my heart could wish for was to be but there again. I stretched out my hands to it, with eager wishes - "O happy desert!" said I, "I shall never see thee more. O miserable creature! whither am going?" Then I reproached myself with my unthankful temper, and that I had repined at my solitary condition; and now what would I give to be on shore there again! Thus, we never see the true state of our condition till it is illustrated to us by its contraries, nor know how to value what we enjoy, but by the want of it.

38. What is the narrator's tone when he states: "It was the 6th of November, in the sixth year of my reign"? **(M)**
    A. sarcastic
    B. mournful
    C. factual
    D. sincere

39. What is the best paraphrase of the following sentence from the last paragraph of the passage: "Then I reproached myself with my unthankful temper, and that I had repined at my solitary condition; and now what would I give to be on shore there again!" **(M)**
    A. I told myself off for being ungrateful about my previous plight.
    B. I considered the bounty to which I had had access, and I regretted that I had felt lonely.
    C. I beat myself up having been ungrateful about being alone because I longed to return to where I was before.
    D. I scolded myself for not appreciating all that I had had before my voyage and for having felt lonely because now I wished that I could go back there again.

40. What can we infer when the narrator states: "we never see the true state of our condition till it is illustrated to us by its contraries"? **(M)**
    A. He misses the life he had before embarking on his journey.
    B. He wishes he could be a more grateful person.
    C. He thinks that others could learn a lesson from his experiences.
    D. We learn who we really are when we feel contrary to others.

READING PRACTICE TEST 2

[1] The question of the mechanics of motion is complex and one that has a protracted history. Indeed, much has been discovered about gravity, defined as the force that draws objects to the earth, both before and since the British mathematician Sir Isaac Newton mused upon the subject in the 17th century. As early as the third century B.C., a Greek philosopher and natural scientist named Aristotle conducted a great deal of scientific investigation into the subject. Most of Aristotle's life was devoted to the study of the objects of natural science, and it is for this work that he is most renowned. The Greek scientist wrote a tome entitled *Metaphysics*, which contains the observations that he made as a result of performing this original research in the natural sciences.

[2] Several centuries later, in the first century AD, Ptolemy, another Greek scientist, was credited with a **nascent**, yet unformulated theory, that there was a force that moved toward the center of the earth, thereby holding objects on its surface. Although later ridiculed for his belief that the earth was the center of the planetary system, **Aristotle's compatriot** nevertheless did contribute to the development of the theory of gravity.

[3] However, it was during the period called the Renaissance that gravitational forces were perhaps studied most widely. An astronomer, Galileo Galilei corrected one of Aristotle's erring theories by pointing out that objects of differing weights fall to earth at the same speed. Years later, Descartes, who was known at that time as a dilettante philosopher, but was later dubbed the father of modern mathematics, held that a body in circular motion constantly strives to recede from the center. This theory gave credence to the notion that bodies in motion had their own forces.

[4] Newton took these studies a step further, and used them to show that the earth's rotation does not fling bodies into the air because the force of gravity, measured by the rate of falling bodies, is greater than the centrifugal force arising from the rotation. In his first mathematical formulation of gravity, published in 1687, Newton posited that the same force that kept the moon from being propelled away from the earth also applied to gravity at the earth's surface. While this finding, termed the Law of Universal Gravitation, is said to have been occasioned by Newton's observation of the fall of an apple from a tree in the orchard at his home, in reality, the idea did not come to the scientist **in a flash of inspiration**, but was developed slowly over time.

[5] Newton's study was of great importance for the scientific community and for society as a whole. It is because of Newton's work that we currently understand the effect of gravity on the earth as a global system. For instance, as a result of Newton's investigation into the subject of gravity, we know today that geological features such as mountains and canyons can cause variances in the Earth's gravitational force. Newton must also be acknowledged for the realization that the force of gravity becomes less robust as the distance from the equator diminishes, due to the rotation of the earth, as well as the declining mass and density of the planet from the equator to the poles.

[6] In spite of these discoveries, Newton remained perplexed throughout his lifetime by the causes of the power implied by the variables of his mathematical equations on gravity. In other words, he was unable adequately to explain the natural forces upon which the power of gravity relied. Even though he tried to justify these forces by describing them merely as phenomena of nature, differing hypotheses on these phenomena still abound today.

[7] In 1915, Albert Einstein addressed Newton's reservations by developing the revolutionary theory of general relativity. Einstein asserted that the paths of objects in motion can sometimes deviate, or change direction over the course of time, as a result of the curvature of space time. Numerous subsequent investigations into and tests of the theory of general relativity have unequivocally supported Einstein's groundbreaking work.

1. Which words mean the same thing as the word "nascent" in paragraph 2? **(M)**
   A. newly formed
   B. old fashioned
   C. widely accepted
   D. obviously untrue

2. The phrase **Aristotle's compatriot** in paragraph 2 refers to: **(M)**
   A. Metaphysics
   B. the planetary system
   C. Ptolemy
   D. an unformulated theory

3. Which of these best explains the phrase "in a flash of inspiration" from paragraph 4? **(D)**
   A. with great inspiration
   B. as though energized
   C. all of a sudden
   D. in the heat of the moment

4. **Part A**
   What is the author's attitude about Newton's achievement? **(D)**
   A. Newton's theories were good for their time, but they have been improved upon.
   B. Newton's discoveries were very meaningful and significant.
   C. Newton should have been able to understand all of the natural forces that he studied.
   D. Newton's reservations provided a good starting point for later researchers.

5. **Part B**
   Which sentence from the article best supports the answer to Part A? **(D)**
   A. Newton's study was of great importance for the scientific community and for society as a whole.
   B. Newton remained perplexed throughout his lifetime by the causes of the power implied by the variables of his mathematical equations on gravity.
   C. Newton must also be acknowledged for the realization that the force of gravity becomes less robust as the distance from the equator diminishes.
   D. He was unable adequately to explain the natural forces upon which the power of gravity relied.

6. How does paragraph 6 contribute to the development of ideas in the article? **(D)**
   A. It emphasizes the significance of Newton's achievement.
   B. It identifies a reservation which Newton experienced.
   C. It analyzes natural phenomena.
   D. It reconciles various gravitational theories.

7. Based on the information contained in paragraph 7, which of the following best explains the term "general relativity"? **(M)**
   A. changes in the motion of objects due to the curved path of space time
   B. the inverse relationship between time and space
   C. the proportionality between paths and objects
   D. the manner in which later researchers supported Einstein

8. According to paragraph 7, what can be inferred about the reaction of the scientific community to Einstein's theory of general relativity? **(M)**
   A. It has received a mixed response.
   B. The response has been overwhelmingly positive.
   C. The reception has been mostly negative.
   D. The scientific community is still undecided about the value of Einstein's work.

[1] Socio-economic status plays a key role in a child's success later in life, rather than intellectual ability, according to a recent study. As an example, let's direct our attention to two elementary school students named Paul and John. Both children are attentive and respectful to their teachers, and both earn good grades. However, Paul's father is an affluent property magnate, while John's dad works on an assembly line in a factory. Even though their academic aptitudes are similar, Paul is 30 times more likely than John to have a high-paying career before reaching his fortieth birthday simply due to the differences in the economic situations of their parents. Indeed, statistics reveal that students like John have a 12% chance of finding and keeping jobs that earn only median-level incomes.

[2] Research dealing with the economics of inequality among adults supports these findings. Importantly, these studies also reveal that the economics of inequality is a trend that has become more and more pronounced in recent years. For instance, in 1960, the mean after-tax pay for a U.S. corporate executive was more than 12 times that of the average factory worker. In 1974, the average CEO's pay had increased to nearly 35 times that of a typical blue-collar worker. By 1980, the situation was even worse: the executive's wages and benefits were nearly 42 times that of the average wage of a factory worker. In the twenty-first century, this situation reached a level which some economists have called hyper-inequality. That is, it is now common for the salary of the average executive to be more than 100 times that of the average factory employee. In fact, in the current year, most CEOs are making, on average, 530 times more than blue-collar employees.

[3] Because of this and other economic dichotomies, a theoretical stance has recently sprung into existence, asserting that inequality is institutionalized. In keeping with this concept, many researchers argue that workers from higher socio-economic backgrounds are disproportionately compensated, even though the contribution they make to society is no more valuable than **that of their lower-paid counterparts**. To rectify the present imbalance caused by this economic stratification, researchers claim that economic rewards should be judged by and distributed according to the worthiness of the employment to society as a whole. Economic rewards under this schema refer not only to wages or salaries, but also to power, status, and prestige within one's community, as well as within larger society.

[4] Recently, cultural and critical theorists have joined in the economic debate that empirical researchers embarked upon decades ago. Focusing on the effect of cultural technologies and systems, they state that various forms of media promote the mechanisms of economic manipulation and oppression. Watching television, they claim, causes those of lower socio-economic class to view themselves as apolitical and powerless victims of the capitalistic machine. Of course, such a phenomenon would have a **deleterious** impact upon individual identity and human motivation.

[5] At a more personal level, economic inequality also has pervasive effects on the lives of the less economically fortunate. These personal effects include the manner in which one's economic status influences musical tastes, the perception of time and space, the expression of emotion, and the communication across social groups. The detrimental economic imbalance may at its most extreme form lead to differences in health and mortality in those from the lower economic levels of society.

[6] While causing problems to many on a personal level, economic inequality is also of concern from a global perspective. The worldwide impact of economic inequality is so severe at present that certain poorer countries are considered to be peripheral during discussions of international monetary policy. In order to solve this problem, many economists believe that consideration must be given not only to political arrangements that make some groups more financially better off than others, but also to the social interaction between people and groups.

[7] Conversely, other theorists argue that financial improvement does not always result in the betterment of any particular society. They point out that levels of personal happiness, as well as trust and cooperation between people, are often highest when monetary considerations within a group are kept to a minimum. Finally, they warn that judgements about any given nation's financial situation may be biased as a result of the Western emphasis on materialism and consumerism.

9. The words **that of their lower-paid counterparts** in the article refer to: **(D)**
   A. the inequality which lower-paid workers encounter
   B. the compensation paid to people of lower-level incomes
   C. the salaries of people from affluent socio-economic strata
   D. the benefit to society from the work of lower compensated people

10. According to paragraph 4, all of the following are accurate statements except: **(M)**
    A. Cultural theorists have expanded upon the work of previous research.
    B. Television and other media have an effect on social inequality.
    C. Television viewing can reinforce feelings of socio-economic subjugation.
    D. People who view television are more motivated to change their lives.

11. Which of the statements below is the best explanation of the following sentence from paragraph 6? **(M)**
    The worldwide impact of economic inequality is so severe at present that certain poorer countries are considered to be peripheral during discussions of international monetary policy.
    A. The influence of poverty has wide-reaching, global implications.
    B. Some countries that are less economically advanced are thought to be irrelevant when debates about worldwide economic protocol take place.
    C. Economic inequality has made certain countries poorer because of debates about international financial matters.
    D. External discussions have increased the severity of worldwide financial inequality.

12. How does the anecdote about John and Paul in paragraph 1 connect to the information in paragraphs 2 and 3? **(D)**
    A. It emphasizes the needs of blue-collar employees.
    B. It portrays a tragic situation that has occurred in the past.
    C. It illustrates the economic effects of social inequality.
    D. It describes how poverty has impacted upon the life of one particular child.

13. **Part A**
    Which statement expresses a claim that the author makes about socio-economic inequality? **(D)**
    A. Socio-economic status has wide-ranging effects on life and lifestyle, as well as on a number of personal preferences and behaviors.
    B. Socio-economic level primarily affects communication skills.
    C. Socio-economic unfairness results predominantly in lethargy among those most profoundly affected by it.
    D. Socio-economic inequality usually results in premature death to those who experience it.

14. **Part B**
    Which sentence from the article best supports the answer to Part A? **(D)**
    A. While causing problems to many on a personal level, economic inequality is also of concern from a global perspective.
    B. At a more personal level, economic inequality also has pervasive effects on the lives of the less economically fortunate.
    C. These personal effects include the manner in which one's economic status influences musical tastes, the perception of time and space, the expression of emotion, and the communication across social groups.
    D. The detrimental economic imbalance may at its most extreme form lead to differences in health and mortality in those from the lower economic levels of society.

15. The word **deleterious** in paragraph 4 is closest in meaning to: **(M)**
    A. motivating
    B. equalizing
    C. injurious
    D. judicious

16. Based on the information in paragraph 7, what can be inferred about the present debate on socio-economic inequality? **(D)**
    A. All theorists agree about the best course of action to take in order to address the issue of economic disparities.
    B. There is unanimous agreement that an improvement in financial conditions leads to an amelioration of other social problems.
    C. There is some dispute surrounding the social and non-monetary effects associated with financial improvement.
    D. Western capitalism serves as the agreed upon, uniform standard towards which all nations should strive.

[1] According to a recent study by the anti-smoking organization Action on Smoking and Health, movie stars who regularly smoke in films are influencing young people to smoke cigarettes. Psychologists believe they have proof that young film viewers are being affected by the image of movie stars with cigarettes between their fingers. While they accept there are limitations to their study, Sally James and her research team stated that their study found a clear link between use of tobacco by movie stars and higher levels of smoking in the teenagers who admire them.

[2] The questionnaire results, which were published today in the magazine *Tobacco Control*, examined 650 students with ages between 10 and 19 from six different schools. They were asked about their smoking behavior, as well as the name of their favorite movie star. The psychologists then evaluated the smoking patterns in recent films of the most popular film stars. They discovered that 65% of these stars smoked on screen at least once and more than 40% depicted smoking as an essential character trait in one or more films. They found that those teenagers who named a favorite film star who had smoked on screen were more likely to smoke or say they wanted to smoke. In addition, the more their film idol smoked on screen, the greater the risk that the young person would become a smoker.

[3] Indeed, the influence of film stars on teenage smoking now has global significance. According to a new World Health Organization (WHO) survey, three out of four films produced by the prolific worldwide film industry over the past decade show stars smoking. Teenagers who watch film characters smoke are three times as likely to do so themselves. If young people see one of their idols light up on-screen they are 16 times more likely to think positively about smoking, the survey found.

[4] It is the first such study of the vast film industry and part of a new international campaign to cut smoking deaths by targeting the world's film industries. The WHO's World No Tobacco Day focuses on how the fashion and film industries glamorize cigarettes. The WHO survey found that 76% of the most popular films produced worldwide within the last ten years showed some form of tobacco use. In 72% of cases, this was cigarette smoking. "The youth thought it was a very cool thing to do." The implication of that is huge," it stated. "Earlier, only the villains were shown smoking, but now there is a very high percentage of the good guys who also smoke in their films. This research shows a clear relation between on-screen tobacco use by movie stars and higher levels of beginning to smoke by the teenagers who admire them," said the researchers.

[5] They also emphasized that there was no evidence that teenagers who already smoked were more interested in the characters who smoked in the films they watched. Instead the association between star smoking and attitudes that predict the chance of starting smoking was even stronger among those teenagers who had never smoked. "This result suggests that the influence of movie star smoking begins before experimenting with cigarettes. We believe this evidence strongly suggests that media portrayals of

tobacco use by popular movie stars contribute to teenage smoking." The results of the study, said the authors, "contribute to a growing body of evidence identifying media exposure to smoking as a major contributing factor in adolescent smoking uptake."

[6] Nevertheless, the film industry is unlikely to react well to the survey. One leading film-maker said tobacco companies, not movie stars, were to blame for teenage smoking.

[7] In addition to the effect that film stars have on adolescents, there may also be other factors that impact upon a teenager's propensity to smoke. Another study suggested that high school children's smoking experiments were strongly influenced by whether they were in a peer group where there were other adolescents who already smoked.

[8] This study, by the Schools Health Education Unit, found that 40% of 12- to 13-year-olds and 60% of 14- to 15-year-olds admitted trying cigarettes last year. This compares to 30% of 12- to 13-year-olds and 57% of 14- to 15-year-olds ten years ago. Smoking among school children has also reached record levels with three-fifths of 14- and 15-year-olds having tried cigarettes. Of the 300,000 young people questioned, more than half lived in a home where at least one person smoked. Some of the teenagers who were surveyed got their cigarettes from parents or older siblings, while others shared the cost of cigarettes with a friend.

[9] Dr. Edward Adams, research manager at the Schools Health Education Unit, expressed alarm about the increasing numbers of children experimenting with smoking. He said: "This is more than just trying a cigarette. The rise in those experimenting with smoking has been matched by an increase in regular smokers as well. Some of them are starting a habit which may go on for years, and the health consequences are very serious."

[10] Scientists had previously assumed addiction did not begin until youths were smoking at least 10 cigarettes a day. However, research which was led by Joseph Difranza demonstrated that the smoking pupils who showed signs of being hooked only had an average of two cigarettes a week. "Some of these kids were hooked within a few days of starting to smoke," said Dr. Difranza. "Data from human and animal studies leads me to suspect that addiction to nicotine begins, in many cases, with the first cigarette." His team suggested that brains of adolescents, because they were still growing, were more vulnerable to addiction. The effect of tobacco might be stronger and longer-lasting than in adults." Youths can get hooked very quickly and at very low levels of nicotine exposure," Dr. Difranza concluded.

17. What is the main idea of paragraphs 1 to 5 of this article? **(M)**
    A. Age limits for viewers have been proposed on films that depict smoking.
    B. The results of a recent survey by Action on Smoking and Health were very surprising.
    C. The film industry's portrayal of smoking has impacted upon adolescent tobacco use.
    D. The process of nicotine addiction occurs quickly in teenagers.

18. What percentage of films produced worldwide in the last ten years depicted tobacco use? **(M)**
    A. 65%
    B. 40%
    C. 76%
    D. 72%

19. Which best summarizes the Focus of WHO's No Tobacco Day? **(M)**
    A. To reveal that tobacco-related illness is geographically disproportionate
    B. To address how tobacco use is portrayed in industries that affect young people
    C. To bring about limitations on cigarette advertising
    D. To publicize the number of tobacco-related deaths

20. **Part A**
    According to the WHO, what was the most significant finding about tobacco use at the time the article was written? **(M)**
    A. Portrayals of tobacco use in movies are more frequent.
    B. The influence of movie star smoking begins before experimenting with cigarettes.
    C. The chance of starting smoking was even stronger among those teenagers who had never smoked.
    D. Smoking in media and film has had an obvious impact on increased levels of teenage smoking.

21. **Part B**
    Which of the following details best supports the answer to Part A? **(M)**
    A. The WHO's World No Tobacco Day focuses on how the fashion and film industries glamorize cigarettes.
    B. It is the first such study of the vast film industry and part of a new international campaign to cut smoking deaths by targeting the world's film industries.
    C. Earlier, only the villains were shown smoking, but now there is a very high percentage of the good guys who also smoke in their films.
    D. This research shows a clear relation between on-screen tobacco use by movie stars and higher levels of beginning to smoke by the teenagers who admire them," said the researchers.

22. According to the article, what three factors most affect an adolescent's desire to smoke? **(D)**
    A. Influence by the tobacco industry
    B. Whether their friends smoke
    C. If they see smoking as something "cool"
    D. Schools Health Education Unit
    E. Whether someone in their home already smokes
    F. The frequency of WHO No Tobacco Day
    G. The cost of cigarettes

23. How does the information provided in paragraph 8 contribute to the development of ideas in the article? **(D)**
    A. It provides important statistics that quantify the author's claims about teenage smoking.
    B. It offers a useful anecdote that casts light on teenage smoking.
    C. It illustrates that teenage smokers live in households with other smokers.
    D. It supports the theories that scientists previously had about addiction.

24. According to Dr. Edward Adams, which one of the following statements is correct? **(M)**
    A. The increase in experimental smoking is less than that of regular smoking.
    B. The increase in experimental smoking is accompanied by an increase in that of regular smoking.
    C. The increase in experimental smoking is more than that of regular smoking.
    D. The increase in experimental smoking is accompanied by a decrease in that of regular smoking.

25. When considering the results of various recent studies, what has caused the most alarm among researchers? **(D)**
    A. The overall rise in teen smoking compared to past adolescent tobacco use.
    B. The fact that teenagers are getting addicted more easily and quickly than before.
    C. The fact that most teen smokers have at least 10 cigarettes a day.
    D. The fact that girls become addicted to smoking much more quickly than boys.

26. Why are teenagers more susceptible to nicotine addiction? **(M)**
    A. Because of peer pressure from their friends
    B. Because of insufficient monitoring at school and at home
    C. Because their brains are not fully developed
    D. Because they had an average of two cigarettes a week

A complex series of interactive patterns govern nearly everything the human body does. We eat to a rhythm and drink, sleep, and even breathe to separate ones. Research shows that the human body clock is affected by three main rhythmic cycles: the rhythm at which the earth revolves on its axis, the monthly revolution of the moon around the earth, and the annual revolution of the earth around the sun.

These rhythms create a sense of time that is both physiological as well as mental. Humans feel hungry about every four hours, sleep about eight hours in every twenty-four-hour period, and dream in cycles of approximately ninety minutes each.

These natural rhythms, sometimes called circadian rhythms, are partially controlled by the hypothalamus in the brain. Circadian rhythms help to explain the "lark vs. owl" hypothesis. Larks are those who quite rightly prefer to rise early in the morning and go to bed early, while owls are those who feel at their best at night and stay up too late.

These cycles explain the phenomenon of jet lag, when the individual's body clock is out of step with the actual clock time in his or her new location in the world. In humans, births and deaths also follow predictable cycles, with most births and deaths occurring between midnight and 6:00 am.

Recently, scientists have also discovered that changes in the body, as well as environmental factors, can cause circadian rhythms to be out of sync. For example, mutations or changes in certain genes can affect a person's biological clock. Research also reveals that light from electronic devices at night can confuse our circadian rhythms.

Changes in circadian rhythms can cause sleep disorders and may lead to other long-term health problems. Obesity, diabetes, seasonal affective disorder, and other mental health issues may result from chronic confusion to one's body clock.

27. In the first paragraph, the author suggests that our mental and physiological sense of time is: **(M)**
    A. appropriate
    B. exaggerated
    C. oversimplified
    D. overgeneralized

28. In the fourth paragraph of the article, the phrase "these cycles" refers to: **(M)**
    A. the "lark vs. owl" hypothesis
    B. circadian rhythms
    C. the hypothalamus in the brain
    D. the individual's body clock

29. **Part A**
    The author's attitude toward those who prefer to retire to bed late in the evening can best be described as one of: **(D)**
    A. disapproval
    B. skepticism
    C. hostility
    D. support

30. **Part B**
Which statement from the article best supports the answer to Part A? **(D)**
   A. Larks are those who quite rightly prefer to rise early in the morning and go to bed early.
   B. Owls are those who feel at their best at night and stay up too late.
   C. Circadian rhythms, are partially controlled by the hypothalamus in the brain.
   D. These rhythms create a sense of time that is both physiological as well as mental.

[1] Although improved weather observation practices seem to have reduced the severity of tornadoes in recent years, they continue to be one of the most severe types of weather-related events. While many people live in fear of tornadoes and the path of destruction they wreak, very few people actually understand how these weather events occur. Even fewer people understand how to protect themselves and their property if a tornado were to strike.

[2] Tornadoes develop as the wind changes direction and the wind speed simultaneously increases. This combination of atmospheric changes results in spinning movements in the troposphere, which is the lowest level of the earth's atmosphere. The resulting whirling motion, which sometimes is not even visible to the observer, is compounded when the rotating air column moves to a vertical position. The developing tornado draws in warm air surrounding it at ground level, and its speed begins to increase. As warm air is drawn in, a funnel is produced that extends from the cloud above it to the earth below. The resulting funnels thus become **pendent** from low-pressure areas of storm clouds.

[3] When a tornado touches the ground, a strong upward draft, which is called a vortex, is formed. The vortex is a circular, rolling column of wind that reaches speeds of more than 200 miles per hour. As it moves across the landscape, the tornado creates a path of destruction. These twisters have been known to lift heavy objects, such as large animals or cars, and cast them off several miles away. Houses that are hit by tornadoes appear to explode as the normal air pressure inside the building collides with the low air pressure inside the vortex.

[4] Tornadoes can appear any time of the year, but they are most common during the summer. Further, while they usually occur between 3:00 PM and 9:00 PM, tornadoes can, in theory, happen at any time of the day. Even though these twisting funnels have been witnessed in many places in the world, they are the most common in the United States. On average, there are 1,200 tornadoes annually in this nation, causing 70 deaths and 1,500 injuries.

[5] In spite of having **myriad** sizes and shapes, tornadoes are normally classified as weak, strong, or violent. It is notable that the majority of all tornadoes are categorized as weak. To be classified as a weak tornado, the duration of the event must be less than 10 minutes and the speed must be under 110 miles per hour. Strong tornadoes, which comprise approximately 10 percent of all twisters, may have durations of more than 20 minutes each and speeds of up to 205 miles per hour. Violent tornadoes are the rarest since they occur less than one percent of the time. Although uncommon, violent tornadoes last for more than one hour and result in the greatest loss of life. While a violent tornado can destroy a solidly-constructed, well-built home, weak tornadoes can also cause a great deal of damage.

[6] Because of the destructive, powerful nature of tornadoes, there are many myths and misconceptions about them. For example, some people hold the view that tornadoes cannot occur over oceans, lakes, or rivers. However, waterspouts, tornadoes that develop over bodies of water, can in many cases cause major damage to coastal areas as they move onshore. Additionally, tornadoes can take place concurrently with tropical storms and hurricanes as they move to land. Another myth is that damage to structures such as office complexes and houses can be prevented if their windows are opened before the storm strikes. Founded on the mistaken belief that open windows can equalize the pressure inside the building and prevent damage to it, this action can instead cause severe injury or death.

[7] Because tornadoes have serious consequences for communities and their inhabitants, safety measures are of the utmost importance during severe weather conditions. Drivers sometimes try to outrun tornadoes in their vehicles, but it is very dangerous to do so. Cars and other vehicles offer very little protection when tornadoes hit, so drivers should leave their vehicles and look for safe shelter. Mobile homes and trailers also afford little shelter, so residents of these types of dwellings should go to an underground floor of the nearest building. In the event that a building has no subterranean level, a person should then find the lowest floor of a nearby building and position him- or herself under a heavy object. If no building is located nearby, a person stuck in a tornado can lie prostrate in a nearby ditch or other low area of land and protect his or her head.

31. The best synonym for the word **pendent** in the article is: **(M)**
    A. churning
    B. increasing
    C. hanging
    D. level

32. All of the following key facts about tornadoes are mentioned in paragraph 4 except: **(M)**
    A. the yearly number of deaths in the US from tornadoes
    B. the time of day when tornadoes usually take place
    C. the time of year when tornadoes are most common
    D. the average wind speed of most tornadoes

33. The word **myriad** in the article is closest in meaning to: **(M)**
    A. limited
    B. extreme
    C. many
    D. average

34. **Part A**
    In paragraph 5, what is the author's main purpose? **(M)**
    A. to explain how tornadoes are classified
    B. to identify the most frequent type of tornadoes
    C. to emphasize the loss of life and damage to property caused by tornadoes
    D. to compare weak tornadoes to strong tornadoes

35. **Part B**
    What detail from the article best supports the answer to Part A? **(M)**
    A. In spite of having myriad sizes and shapes, tornadoes are normally classified as weak, strong, or violent.
    B. It is notable that the majority of all tornadoes are categorized as weak.
    C. Although uncommon, violent tornadoes last for more than one hour and result in the greatest loss of life.
    D. While a violent tornado can destroy a solidly-constructed, well-built home, weak tornadoes can also cause a great deal of damage.

36. How does the information contained in paragraph 6 connect to the assertions made in paragraph 1? **(D)**
    A. It shows that tornadoes can move away from coastal areas.
    B. It provides a further example of the misinformation that people have about tornadoes.
    C. It supports the idea that tornadoes are powerful and destructive.
    D. It reveals that tornadoes can accompany tropical storms and hurricanes.

37. **Part A**
    According to paragraphs 6 and 7, what can be inferred about the public's knowledge about tornadoes? **(M)**
    A. A large number of people know how to avoid tornado damage.
    B. Most people appreciate the risk of death associated with tornadoes.
    C. Some members of the public know how to regulate the pressure inside buildings.
    D. A number of people are not fully aware of certain key information about tornadoes, especially about tornado safety.

38. **Part B**
    What sentence from the article best supports the answer to Part A? **(M)**
    A. Another myth is that damage to structures such as office complexes and houses can be prevented if their windows are opened before the storm strikes.
    B. Because tornadoes have serious consequences for communities and their inhabitants, safety measures are of the utmost importance during severe weather conditions.
    C. Drivers sometimes try to outrun tornadoes in their vehicles, but it is very dangerous to do so.
    D. Mobile homes and trailers also afford little shelter, so residents of these types of dwellings should go to an underground floor of the nearest building.

39. According to the article, tornadoes are considered to be a severe weather phenomenon because: **(M)**
    A. many people fear them.
    B. they produce strong vortexes.
    C. they can be placed into three discrete categories.
    D. they can result in death and devastation

40. Select the answer below that represents the two most important ideas contained in the article. **(D)**
    A. (i) Tornadoes can cause catastrophic loss in terms of life and property.
       (ii) Everyone should be educated about what to do in the event of a tornado.
    B. (i) Most tornadoes occur in the afternoon.
       (ii) Few tornadoes are violent.
    C. (i) Some members of the public are ill-informed about when and where tornadoes can occur.
       (ii) Sheltering in a ditch is a last resort if a tornado should strike.
    D. (i) Most tornadoes occur in the afternoon.
       (ii) Everyone should be educated about what to do in the event of a tornado.

READING PRACTICE TEST 3

[1] Adventurers, fieldwork assistants, and volunteers are gradually replacing tourists. Still, the classification 'tourist' will never totally disappear. There might still be those who wish to travel to foreign lands for their own enjoyment, but doing so will be a **clandestine** and frowned-upon activity. No one will admit to belonging to that category.

[2] Burma and Bali have recently prohibited tourists from entering parts of their countries. The list of places that tourists cannot explore is ever-expanding. The international tourist organization Tourism Concern states that Belize, Botswana, China, East Africa, Peru, Thailand, and Zanzibar all have areas that have been adversely impacted upon by tourism. Representatives from Tourism Concern believe that tourists are destroying the environment, as well as local cultures. These representatives also assert that although tourists bring money to the countries they visit, they must be stopped at any price.

[3] **These notions** may seem ironic since tourism was unquestionably encouraged as something that was inherently good a few decades ago. The advent of relatively less expensive accommodation and flights has meant that tourism can finally be enjoyed by the majority of the population. The United Nations declared the year 1967 "The International Year of the Tourist," and during the twenty-first century, more and more families are traveling abroad on family vacations.

[4] The World Tourism Organization (WTO) has predicted that by the year 2050, there will be 1.56 billion tourists per year traveling somewhere in the world. This forecast demonstrates the immense challenge in trying to curb the global demand for tourism. In fact, the task may be so tremendous that it might just be impossible.

[5] Some argue that the government should intervene, but the government alone would face huge impediments in attempting to make so many economically-empowered people stop doing something that they enjoy. Others assert that tourism is of such extreme damage to the welfare of the world that only totally irresponsible individuals would ever consider doing it. Yet, this argument is clearly absurd. Whatever benefits or otherwise accrue from tourism, it is not evil, despite what a tiny minority might say. It can cause harm. It can be neutral, and it can occasionally bring about something good.

[6] As a result, tourism is under attack by more a more oblique method: it has been re-named. Bit by bit, the word "tourist" is being removed from the tourism industry.

[7] Since tourism has changed, so too must the vacation. Adventurers, fieldwork assistants, and volunteers do not go on vacations. These new travelers go on "cultural experiences", "expeditions" or "projects". However, re-branding tourism in this way gives freedom to travelers, as well as restrictions.

[8] The various booklets, pamphlets, and brochures distributed by the new industry for travelers are now attempting to **emulate** advertisements produced by charities. For example, *Global Adventure* magazine produces an annual "99 Great Adventures Guide" which mixes charitable expeditions with vacations as if the two things are one and the same.

[9] New travelers express great interest in respecting the environments they visit. They avoid tourist infrastructures because they are afraid of being viewed negatively by the local culture. Instead, they prefer accommodation arrangements such as cabins or camping. These types of accommodation, they believe, are more respectful of local culture. Local culture is very important to the new tourist, whereas the mass tourist is believed to destroy it.

[10] Nevertheless, all types of tourism should be responsible towards and respectful of environmental and human resources. Some tourism developers, as well as individual tourists, have not acted with this in mind. Consequently, a divide is being driven between those few affluent and privileged tourists and the remaining majority.

1. **Part A**
   What is the best title for this article? **(M)**
   A. Tourism and the Environment
   B. Adventurers, Tourists, and Travelers
   C. The Changing Face of Tourism
   D. Tourism: Its Advantages and Disadvantages

2. **Part B**
   Which sentence from the article best supports the answer to Part A? **(M)**
   A. Burma and Bali have recently prohibited tourists from entering parts of their countries.
   B. The World Tourism Organization (WTO) has predicted that by the year 2050, there will be 1.56 billion tourists per year traveling somewhere in the world.
   C. As a result, tourism is under attack by more a more oblique method: it has been re-named.
   D. Local culture is very important to the new tourist, whereas the mass tourist is believed to destroy it.

3. The word **clandestine** in the article is closest in meaning to: **(M)**
   A. distressing
   B. secret
   C. pleasurable
   D. difficult

4. The author mentions all off the following facts about tourism in paragraphs 2 and 3 except: **(M)**
   A. the names of certain countries that have banned tourists.
   B. the names of countries that have been negatively affected by tourism.
   C. the reasons why flights became inexpensive.
   D. the reasons why new views on tourism may seem paradoxical when compared to views on tourism in the past.

5. The word **emulate** in the article is closest in meaning to: **(M)**
   A. strive
   B. utilize
   C. imitate
   D. distribute

6. The words **these notions** in the article refer to: **(M)**
   A. The way that tourists bring money to the countries they visit.
   B. The manner in which tourism helps local cultures.
   C. The fact that tourism used to be encouraged as something good.
   D. The viewpoints that express disdain for tourism.

7. How does the mention of "cultural experiences," "expeditions," or "projects" in paragraph 7 connect to the assertion in paragraph 6? **(D)**
   A. It exemplifies how tourists respect the environment.
   B. It contradicts the evidence in support of advertising.
   C. It illustrates how tourism has been re-branded.
   D. It argues that charitable expeditions are now indistinguishable from vacations.

8. **Part A**
   Which of the following best expresses the author's attitude towards the past effects of tourism on the environment? **(D)**
   A. regrettable
   B. capricious
   C. unclear
   D. uncertain

9. **Part B**
   Which sentence from the article best supports the answer to Part A? **(D)**
   A. Local culture is very important to the new tourist, whereas the mass tourist is believed to destroy it.
   B. Nevertheless, all types of tourism should be responsible towards and respectful of environmental and human resources.
   C. Some tourism developers, as well as individual tourists, have not acted with this in mind.
   D. Consequently, a divide is being driven between those few affluent and privileged tourists and the remaining majority.

[1] Every morning, tens of thousands of children under age ten have nothing to eat or drink before leaving home for school. Research also shows that out of all youths in the 13-year-old age group, 7% are regular smokers. In addition, the consumption of alcoholic beverages in the 11-to-15-year-old age group has more than doubled in the past decade, with 25% of this age group drinking on average the equivalent of over four cans of beer every week.

[2] In spite of an overall trend for improvements in child health, inequalities in health have been on the rise. A significant aspect of health inequalities is that rates of disease and death are far higher in poorer households. One key reason for tackling the issue of child poverty is to rectify in particular the inequalities in child health, which will otherwise carry over into adulthood. Accordingly, the government has made the commitment to attempt to lower child poverty dramatically in the next two decades.

[3] But will the government's commitment actually reduce child poverty and improve child health? Cynics say that the government's monetary support for poor households will invariably be spent on consumables like candy and potato chips, or other junk food, or worse, on tobacco, alcohol, and even drugs. Realistically, however, providing households with more money in the form of governmental assistance should give them the opportunity to spend more money on nutritious, often more expensive, food.

[4] Yet, if the government truly wishes to improve the health of poor children, it should realize that families cannot rely on only modest increases in income. For the children leaving home without any breakfast, these government measures are not enough. A better option would be to feed **these children** through school breakfast and dinner programs.

[5] In fact, research demonstrates that children's concentration and learning suffer when they do not have a nutritious breakfast. In response to this research, some countries have developed programs for nutritious school breakfasts and dinners, and **they** have allocated more funds to these meal programs than to welfare benefits. There remains a clear need for the authorities to address nutrition as one of the worst symptoms of child poverty since disadvantaged children in many areas still do not get a nourishing breakfast and the effectiveness of their education is jeopardized as a result.

[6] Smoking also greatly damages the health of children and increases childhood mortality rates. While the government has raised the cigarette tax, thereby increasing the cost of tobacco to consumers, this has not brought about the desired result. On the contrary, it has left poor parents who smoke worse off, and their children will continue to suffer. Children's health would be better served if the government allocated funds to preventing cigarette sales to children, instead of the hefty monetary resources spent on attempting to halt cigarette smuggling and related tax evasion.

[7] Children, particularly young adolescents, are also sickly because of the ever-increasing consumption of alcohol in this age group. One reason for the rise in children's drinking is the increase in the availability of sweetened bottled alcoholic drinks. These beverages make alcohol more attractive and more appealing to young people and children. Nevertheless, the government appears be in something of a quandary, perhaps wishing to speak out against major beverage manufacturing companies, and yet succumbing to lobbying by and accepting related financial support from big businesses like Anheuser-Busch.

[8] Improving children's opportunities depends on ending child poverty and improving the health of the poorest children. While these goals are related, it would be foolish to believe that the reduction of child poverty would automatically improve children's nutrition and reduce their smoking and drinking. Re-thinking the allocation of governmental funds to nutrition and effective education and prevention about addiction are still needed in order to improve child health.

10. **Part A**
    What is the author's primary purpose in this article? **(D)**
    A. To decry poor child health and point the finger at the primary culprits
    B. To demonstrate that child health would automatically improve if certain solutions were to be carried out
    C. To enumerate the reasons for health inequalities, particularly in children, and to allude to some possible courses of action
    D. To demonstrate the reasons why the consumption of alcohol and tobacco are harmful for children

11. **Part B**
    Which sentence from the article best supports the answer to Part A? **(D)**
    A. Research also shows that out of all youths in the 13-year-old age group, 7% are regular smokers.
    B. In addition, the consumption of alcoholic beverages in the 11-to-15-year-old age group has more than doubled in the past decade, with 25% of this age group drinking on average the equivalent of over four cans of beer every week.
    C. If the government truly wishes to improve the health of poor children, it should realize that families cannot rely on only modest increases in income.
    D. Improving children's opportunities depends on ending child poverty and improving the health of the poorest children.

12. According to paragraph 1, the following statements are true except: **(M)**
    A. Many young children regularly go to school on an empty stomach.
    B. Alcohol consumption has risen across many age groups in the last ten years.
    C. Children as young as thirteen years old have developed smoking habits.
    D. Twenty-five percent of a certain age group regularly consumes alcohol every week.

13. The word **they** highlighted in paragraph 5 refers to: **(M)**
    A. countries that have established school breakfasts.
    B. children who regularly do not receive breakfast.
    C. researchers in the field of child nutrition.
    D. fund-raisers for school meal programs.

14. Which of the statements below best explains the following sentence from paragraph 5? **(M)**
    There remains a clear need for the authorities to address nutrition as one of the worst symptoms of child poverty since disadvantaged children in many areas still do not get a nourishing breakfast and the effectiveness of their education is jeopardized as a result.
    - A. The government needs to provide nourishing breakfasts to children so that they can improve their learning.
    - B. Poor children do not start the day with a good meal and cannot learn well as a result, so it is of the utmost importance for the government to improve child poverty and child nutrition.
    - C. Child poverty continues to be a grave social problem and nutrition is a concomitant issue; therefore, the government should get involved.
    - D. Poor nutrition is one aspect of poverty and increased government funds need to be set aside to deal with this situation.

15. Why does the author discuss smoking in paragraph 6 of the article? **(D)**
    - A. To establish the link between cigarette smuggling and tax evasion
    - B. To exemplify how poor parents who smoke will continue to do so, exacerbating their children's health problems
    - C. To enumerate details about a government policy
    - D. To expand on another aspect of poor health in children

16. **Part A**
    What does the author suggest about the government's reluctance to criticize the practices of big businesses? **(D)**
    - A. It is loath to lose the monetary support that large beverage companies have to offer.
    - B. It realizes that there is no reason to reduce the demand for certain alcoholic drinks.
    - C. It wishes to reduce its reliance on financing from lobbyists.
    - D. It understands that doing so would not make alcohol less attractive to youngsters.

17. **Part B**
    What detail from the article best supports the answer to Part A? **(D)**
    - A. Children's health would be better served if the government allocated funds to preventing cigarette sales to children.
    - B. One reason for the rise in children's drinking is the increase in the availability of sweetened bottled alcoholic drinks.
    - C. These beverages make alcohol more attractive and more appealing to young people and children.
    - D. Nevertheless, the government appears be in something of a quandary, perhaps wishing to speak out against major beverage manufacturing companies, and yet succumbing to lobbying by and accepting related financial support from big businesses like Anheuser-Busch.

18. Based on the information in paragraph 8, which statement best describes the relationship between the goals of improved opportunities for children and the problems of child poverty and ill health? **(D)**
    - A. The reduction of governmental reliance on large companies is inextricably intertwined with the goal of improving children's opportunities.
    - B. The government needs to re-evaluate its relationship to lobbyists if it is ever going to solve the issue of poor child health.
    - C. Establishing the goal of addressing of child poverty will dramatically improve children's health and opportunities, but it may take an extended time period to do so.
    - D. The achievement of the goal of the reduction of child poverty would improve child health and increase the opportunities of children to some extent, but it would not entirely eradicate the problem.

[1] Results of a survey on social trends have identified a rise in immigration as the most significant social change in recent years. Homegrown population increases, defined as the surplus of births over deaths, have been surpassed by immigration. In other words, immigration has increased, while natural population growth has fallen. Specifically, at the end of the twentieth century, net inward migration increased, while natural population growth fell. This amounted to a shift in the significance of immigration to changes in the population, with consequences for ethnic mix and structure. Population patterns have changed dramatically as immigration has become the main **catalyst** for population growth. Moreover, migration patterns within the country appear to be closely linked to where and how people choose to live.

[2] In spite of **this steady influx** of new members of the population, most people regard immigration as a very good thing which benefits the country. These benefits include the skills brought by workers that are needed to expand the information technology industry. The younger age profile of immigrants also helps to balance the pressures of an aging population.

[3] The survey also revealed other important social trends relating to immigration and population. Notably, the population tripled from almost 76 million at the beginning of the twentieth century to nearly 281 million at the start of the twenty-first century. Average household size declined by 2 people per household over the last century, from 4.6 people per household a hundred years ago to 2.6 members per household today. Population density has increased two-fold during the last one hundred years, but remains relatively low in comparison to most other countries in the world. Alaska had the lowest population density, and the population density of the Northeast, which has always been high, continued consistently to outstrip that of other regional areas. While most of the population lived outside cities prior to the end of World War II, the percentage of the population living in metropolitan areas increased in every subsequent decade of the study. New York and California had the largest populations, and Florida and Arizona had the fastest-growing populations during the period of the study.

[4] Until 1970, the majority of households were living in the Northeast and Midwest, but since 1980, the majority was in the South and West. Slightly more than half of all households are now maintained by people aged 45 and over. Female householders have increased as a proportion of all householders, and older females were far more likely to live alone than were men or younger women. The per capita marriage rate has fallen in the last fifteen years, and there was a concurrent drop in the per capita divorce rate during this time.

[5] The survey also examined changes to overall national income, as well as the spending habits of individuals and households. It has found that the distribution of income has become more and more unequal over the past forty years, with the income of the richest 10% of the people in the country rising disproportionately to that of the poorest sector of the population. As relatively worse-off households struggle to make essential purchases, the amount of consumer credit has increased to over a trillion dollars, with credit cards and revolving credit arrangements constituting **the lion's share of** this figure. Cash transactions fell sharply as innovative technologies and new forms of payment appeared in the marketplace.

19. The word **catalyst** in this article is closest in meaning to: **(D)**
    A. resource
    B. reference
    C. reason
    D. result

20. The words **this steady influx** in this article refer to: **(D)**
    A. the consistent improvement in ethnic diversity in the population.
    B. the constant increase in people coming to the country for the first time.
    C. the continual stream of benefits and skills brought by new workers.
    D. the gradual expansion in the technology sector.

21. According to paragraph 3, what was the most notable change to the population in the last one hundred years? **(D)**
    A. The three-fold increase in the size of the population
    B. The increase in average household size
    C. The worryingly high rise in population density
    D. The low population density in Alaska

22. How does the mention of the changes to the populations of Florida and Arizona in paragraph 3 relate to the other information in the article? **(D)**
    A. It points out that new residents are continually moving to these states, which is an aspect of population change.
    B. It contrasts their population changes to those in New York and California, and underscores the notion of migration.
    C. It exemplifies the increase in the percentage of the population living in metropolitan areas.
    D. It illustrates why people wish to leave the Northeast and Midwest, which has affected population density.

23. Which of these best explains the meaning of the phrase "the lion's share of" in paragraph 5? **(D)**
    A. the background to something
    B. an indebtedness to something
    C. the majority of something
    D. a fluctuating part of something

24. Which of the following statements expresses a possible interpretation of the relationship between the changes to the marriage rate and divorce rate? **(D)**
    A. The marriage rate went down because more women preferred to live alone.
    B. The divorce rate went down because fewer people got married during the period of the study.
    C. The marriage rated went down because the core of the population is aging.
    D. The divorce rate declined because existing marriages became more stable.

25. **Part A**
    Based on the information contained in the article, what could be inferred about the reason why female householders increased as a proportion of all householders? **(A)**
    A. Women are preoccupied about the needs of their children, so they deprioritize other relationships.
    B. Women generally suffer from a decline in household income after the breakup of a relationship.
    C. Women are more likely to live alone after losing a life partner than men are.
    D. The social stigma of divorce is greater for women than men.

26. **Part B**
    Which detail from the passage best supports the answer to Part A? **(A)**
    A. Female householders have increased as a proportion of all householders.
    B. Older females were far more likely to live alone than were men or younger women.
    C. The per capita marriage rate has fallen in the last fifteen years, and there was a concurrent drop in the per capita divorce rate during this time.
    D. It has found that the distribution of income has become more and more unequal over the past forty years.

27. Summarize the article by selecting the group of sentences below that express the three most important ideas contained in it: **(D)**
    A. (i) The population has increased as a result of immigration.
       (ii) There were notable changes in the concentration of the population in certain states and geographic regions.
       (iii) The distribution of income has become increasingly skewed in favor of the rich.
    B. (i) The population has increased due to increased birth rates and rising immigration.
       (ii) There were notable changes in the concentration of the population in certain states and geographic regions.
       (iii) The distribution of income has become increasingly skewed in favor of the rich.
    C. (i) There were notable changes in the concentration of the population in certain states and geographic regions.
       (ii) Marriage and divorce rates have fallen.
       (iii) The distribution of income has become increasingly skewed in favor of the rich.
    D. (i) There were notable changes in the concentration of the population in certain states and geographic regions.
       (ii) The distribution of income has become increasingly skewed in favor of the rich.
       (iii) More and more women prefer to live alone.

The Earth's only natural satellite, the Moon lacks its own atmosphere and is only about one-fourth the size of the planet it orbits. The equality of its orbital rate to that of the Earth is the result of gravitational locking, also known as synchronous rotation. Thus, the same hemisphere of the Moon always faces the earth.

The brightest lunar surface areas are formed from meteoric material, while its dark surface regions, called mare basalts or basaltic plains, are the result of volcanic flooding related to impacts from asteroids. Scientific dating of samples from the Moon's crust reveals that the materials range in age from three to four billion years old.

Lunar evolution models suggest that the development of the Moon occurred in five principle stages: (1) increase in mass followed by large-scale melting; (2) separation of the crust with concurrent bombardment by meteors; (3) melting at greater depth; (4) lessening of meteoric bombardment with further melting at depth and the formation of basaltic plains; and (5) the cessation of volcanic activity followed by gradual internal cooling.

The geological and mineral composition of the surface of the Moon seems to mimic that of Earth. Accordingly, one popular theory hypothesizes that the Moon grew out of debris that was dislodged from the Earth's crust following the impact of a large object with the planet.

28. For which of the following situations does the concept of synchronous rotation, as it is defined in the article, provide the most likely explanation? **(A)**
    A. The Moon goes through four phases every twenty-eight days.
    B. A star appears to shine at the same intensity, regardless of its position in the sky.
    C. Two objects fall to the ground at the same speed and land at the same time.
    D. A telecommunications satellite is always in the same position above a certain city on Earth.

29. The article suggests that which one of the following probably occurred after the completion of the process of lunar evolution? **(D)**
    A. Ice continued to melt on the surface of the Moon.
    B. The likelihood of the collision of the Moon with a meteor was substantially reduced.
    C. Melting at depth still occurred.
    D. The temperature of the internal core of the Moon was lower than it was previously.

30. Which of the following, if true, would tend to disprove the hypothesis that the Moon grew out of debris that was dislodged from the Earth's crust? **(A)**
    A. An analysis reveals that there are no geological similarities between samples of material from the surface of the Moon and material from the Earth's crust.
    B. The Moon has been found not to have had any previous volcanic activity.
    C. Many meteors bombarded with the Earth during the process of lunar evolution.
    D. A great deal of debris is created when a meteor collides with the Earth.

It was the last day of July. The long hot summer was drawing to a close; and we, the weary pilgrims of the London pavement, were beginning to think of the cloud-shadows on the corn-fields, and the autumn breezes on the sea-shore.

For my own poor part, the fading summer left me out of health and out of spirits. During the past year I had not managed my professional resources as carefully as usual; and my extravagance now limited me to the prospect of spending the autumn economically between my mother's cottage at Hampstead and my own chambers in town.

The evening, I remember, was still and cloudy. It was one of the two evenings in every week which I was accustomed to spend with my mother and my sister. So I turned my steps northward in the direction of Hampstead.

The quiet twilight was still trembling on the topmost ridges of the heath; and the view of London below me had sunk into a black gulf in the shadow of the cloudy night, when I stood before the gate of my mother's cottage. I had hardly rung the bell before the house door was opened violently; my worthy Italian friend, Professor Pesca, appeared in the servant's place; and darted out joyously to receive me, with a shrill foreign parody on an English cheer.

I had first become acquainted with my Italian friend by meeting him at certain great houses where he taught his own language and I taught drawing. All I then knew of the history of his life was, that he had once held a situation in the University of Padua; that he had left Italy for political reasons (the nature of which he uniformly declined to mention to any one); and that he had been for many years respectably established in London as a teacher of languages.

I had seen him risk his life in the sea at Brighton. We had met there accidentally, and were bathing together. It never occurred to me that the art which we were practicing might merely add one more to the list of manly exercises which the Professor believed that he could learn impromptu.

31. What does the narrator suggest in paragraph 2? **(D)**
    A. that he has run out of money
    B. that he has lost all his clients
    C. that he is suffering from depression
    D. that he does not get along well with his mother

32. Why does the narrator mention his mother and sister in paragraph 3? **(D)**
    A. to imply that Hampstead is in a poorer part of the city
    B. to foreshadow the events that will take place in his mother's cottage
    C. to indicate a routine
    D. to create a contrast with Professor Pesca

33. What is the best paraphrase of the following phrase from paragraph 4?: "appeared in the servant's place." **(D)**
    A. rang the bell for the doorman
    B. did the job of the doorman
    C. stood where the servant normally stands
    D. received the servant's guests

34. What adjective best describes the narrator's relationship with Professor Pesca? **(M)**
    A. political
    B. respectable
    C. accidental
    D. collegial

35. What does the narrator state or imply in the last paragraph? **(M)**
    A. Professor Pesca saved someone who was drowning.
    B. Professor Pesca was not prone to impulsive actions.
    C. Professor Pesca did not know how to swim.
    D. Professor Pesca had experience working with the Coast Guard.

Clare, restless, went out into the dusk when evening drew on, she who had won him having retired to her chamber. The night was as sultry as the day. There was no coolness after dark unless on the grass. Roads, garden-paths, the house-fronts, the bartonwalls were warm as earths, and reflected the noontime temperature into the **noctambulist's** face.

He sat on the east gate of the yard, and knew not what to think of himself. Feeling had indeed smothered judgement that day. Since the sudden embrace, three hours before, the twain had kept apart. She seemed stilled, almost alarmed, at what had occurred, while the novelty, unpremeditation, mastery of circumstance disquieted him—palpitating, contemplative being that he was. He could hardly realize their true relations to each other as yet, and what their mutual bearing should be before third parties thenceforward.

The windows smiled, the door coaxed and beckoned, the creeper blushed confederacy. A personality within it was so far-reaching in her influence as to spread into and make the bricks, mortar, and whole overhanging sky throb with a burning sensibility. Whose was this mighty personality? A milkmaid's.

It was amazing, indeed, to find how great a matter the life of this place had become to him. And though new love was to be held partly responsible for this, it was not solely so. Many have learnt that the magnitude of lives is not as to their external displacements, but as to their subjective experiences. The impressionable peasant leads a larger, fuller, more dramatic life than the king. Looking at it thus, he found that life was to be seen of the same magnitude here as elsewhere.

Despite his heterodoxy, faults, and weaknesses, Clare was a man with a conscience. Tess was no insignificant creature to toy with and dismiss; but a woman living her precious life—a life which, to herself who endured or enjoyed it, possessed as great a dimension as the life of the mightiest to himself. Upon her sensations the whole world depended to Tess; through her existence all her fellow-creatures existed, to her. The universe itself only came into being for Tess on the particular day in the particular year in which she was born.

36. The bartonwalls mentioned in paragraph 1 are most likely: **(D)**
    A. an area in the garden.
    B. a feature of the natural landscape.
    C. a part of the house.
    D. a path leading to one of the roads.

37. What is the meaning of the word "noctambulist" as it is used in paragraph 1? **(D)**
    A. a person who suddenly falls in love
    B. a person who responds impulsively to subjective experiences
    C. a person who experiences an external displacement
    D. a person who goes for a walk after dark

38. What is the best paraphrase of the following statement from paragraph 2: "what their mutual bearing should be before third parties thenceforward"? **(D)**
    A. how they should behave to each other around other people
    B. whether or not they should support each other as a couple from this moment onwards
    C. whether or not they should kiss each other in public
    D. how they should decide whom to tell that they are now a couple

39. Where does the story take place? **(D)**
    A. in a royal court
    B. in a peasant's abode
    C. in a dairy farm
    D. in a manor house

40. What does the narrator imply when he states that "Clare was a man with a conscience"? **(D)**
    A. Clare has behaved poorly towards women in the past, but he repents of this behavior.
    B. Clare knows that Tess is hypersensitive, but she has to be aware of his needs.
    C. Clare understands that his life in his current environment may not be of the same magnitude that he has experienced in the past.
    D. Clare realizes that he needs to treat Tess well because she has had her own life experiences, both positive and negative.

READING PRACTICE TEST 4

Note: All of the questions in this practice test are advanced **(A).**

[1] Do you believe in the saying, "You reap what you sow"? This old adage may mean nothing to some people, but businesses who fail to heed this advice do so at their peril. Of course, it is a well-known fact that no business can start making money without investing some money first. Businesses need to secure licenses. Money is needed just to establish a business, from the planning down to the last details. And even if a business is already established in the market, still, it will need money to invest in new product and technology development.

[2] Statistical reports show that most businesses spend more than $100 million just to build up and introduce a new consumer product in the United States. More than $200 million is needed to embark on and launch a new pharmaceutical product.

[3] Hence, if a business does not have money at its incipience, it will be impossible for the business to grow. So, businesses that seek to develop new business ideas or product development concepts will certainly fail if they don't borrow the money to do so.

[4] Generally, many business owners will run to their family, relatives, or friends to get financial backup or investment. Others would turn to financial institutions such as banks or lending companies. As much as these funding sources can help new projects, they may be inadequate, or businesses may be charged higher interest rates, which, in turn, will put a financial risk on a fledging business, especially if it is trying to develop new products.

[5] For this reason, the government offers financial help to businesses seeking to develop new products or inventions. Government grants are one of the most efficient financial alternatives available for businesses. Even if it requires a heavy burden in terms of paperwork, the benefit of the support obtained will far outweigh the bureaucratic inconvenience.

[6] The government is willing to support those businesses that continuously evolve into a more progressive industry by developing and entertaining new industrial and technological concepts. The government seeks to help those businesses that, in spite of the limited resources, can develop innovations and launch them into the marketplace. By doing so, the government believes that ideas like these can, likewise, help them develop and expand the U.S. economy. **That is the unstated subtext of this program.**

[7] In the United States, the government devotes approximately $70 billion each year towards subsidizing development and research projects. Both the state and federal governments are dedicated to promoting and cultivating inventive projects. For this reason, the government had created various assistance and programs to finance the growth of new technologies.

[8] Among the many government programs, Small Business Innovation Research, or the SBIR, provides an important service because it mainly focuses on small businesses. Through the government's Small Business Innovation Research Program, small businesses are supported and encouraged to delve into their technological capabilities.

[9] With this program, the government provides financial enticements to small businesses to engage in research and development and to make state-of-the-art improvements in the technological arena. The government, likewise, benefits from these innovations as it gains technological and consumerist clout. Through this program, the government grants financial support up to as much as one billion dollars a year to small businesses in the United States.

[10] So, business that are struggling with product development have many solutions at hand. Fledging businesses should seek government assistance to help them expand, improve, and develop.

1. **Part A**
    The main problem the author addresses is that new small businesses in the United States:
    A. are crippled by the cost of securing licenses.
    B. often fail to plan the small details that are necessary for their success.
    C. lack the money they need to devote to product and technology development.
    D. sometimes need to turn to friends and family members for financial assistance.

2. **Part B**
    Which detail from the article best supports the answer to Part A?
    A. As much as these funding sources can help new projects, they may be inadequate, or businesses may be charged higher interest rates, which, in turn, will put a financial risk on a fledging business, especially if it is trying to develop new products.
    B. In the United States, the government devotes approximately $70 billion each year towards subsidizing development and research projects.
    C. Through the government's Small Business Innovation Research Program, small businesses are encouraged to delve into their technological capabilities.
    D. Although the SBIR is a general funding program of the US government, each department in the US government has their own SBIR program.

3. Read the sentence from paragraph 3.

    So, businesses that seek to develop new business ideas or product development concepts will certainly fail if they don't borrow the money to do so.

    Which key idea does the sentence support?
    A. The government offers financial assistance to small businesses.
    B. It is impossible for businesses to expand without outside financial assistance.
    C. The expansion of business and technology helps the economy.
    D. THE SBIR is an important service for small businesses.

4. **Part A**
    Which statement represents a claim made by the author in paragraph 5?
    A. The government operates with efficiency in business matters.
    B. The government overwhelms grant applicants with red tape.
    C. Businesses would be foolish not to seek support from the government.
    D. The advantages of seeking business financial assistance from the government outweigh the disadvantages.

5. **Part B**
    Which detail from the article best supports the answer to Part A?
    A. For this reason, the government offers financial help to businesses seeking to develop new products or inventions.
    B. Government grants are one of the most efficient financial alternatives available for businesses.
    C. Even if it requires a heavy burden in terms of paperwork, the benefit of the support obtained will far outweigh the bureaucratic inconvenience.
    D. The government is willing to support those businesses that continuously evolve into a more progressive industry by developing and entertaining new industrial and technological concepts.

6. Which one these best explains the meaning of the sentence: "That is the unstated subtext of this program"?
   A. That is why the program is popular.
   B. That is why the government wishes to obscure the true reason for technological advancement.
   C. That is why the government is willing to help those kinds of businesses.
   D. That is why certain businesses have limited financial resources to devote to the research and development of technological innovations.

7. **Part A**
   Which statement explains how paragraphs 6 and 7 support the author's claim that business development helps the United States as a whole?
   A. The paragraphs suggest that business development improves the national economy.
   B. The paragraphs suggest that the government should eventually withdraw support from businesses.
   C. The paragraphs suggest that business development will make the marketplace more competitive.
   D. The paragraphs suggest that subsidies will increase in the future.

8. **Part B**
   Which sentence from the article best supports the answer to Part A?
   A. The government seeks to help those businesses that, in spite of the limited resources, can develop innovations and launch them into the marketplace.
   B. By doing so, the government believes that ideas like these can, likewise, help them develop and expand the U.S. economy.
   C. In the United States, the government devotes approximately $70 billion each year towards subsidizing development and research projects.
   D. Both the state and federal governments are dedicated to promoting and cultivating inventive projects.

9. **Part A**
   Which statement describes how the author explains the involvement of the SBIR with small businesses?
   A. The SBIR is supported by both state and federal governments.
   B. The SBIR mandates small businesses to enter the technology sector.
   C. The SBIR offers financial assistance to certain small businesses.
   D. The SBIR has one billion dollars to offer small businesses.

10. **Part B**
    Which sentence from the article best supports the answer to Part A?
    A. Among the many government programs, Small Business Innovation Research, or the SBIR, provides an important service because it mainly focuses on small businesses.
    B. With this program, the government provides financial enticement to small businesses to engage in research and development and to make state-of-the-art improvements in the technological arena.
    C. The government, likewise, benefits from these innovations as it gains technological and consumerist clout.
    D. Fledging businesses should seek government assistance to help them expand, improve, and develop.

[1] Scientists have been able to clone mice for the very first time by using stem cells harvested from the hairs of mature animals. The procedure is much more efficient than cloning with the use of adult cells, and it could be used to create individualized therapies for those suffering from Alzheimer's and Parkinson's diseases. In the past, mice had been cloned with the use of adult cells, but it was a very inefficient process.

[2] In the long term, scientists want to use such legalized cloning to generate therapies. A patient's skin cell could generate a cloned embryo which is grown for just a few days, at which point it is the size of a pin head. If embryonic stem cells, which can turn into any type of tissue, were harvested from the early-stage embryo they could be used to regenerate damaged tissue which is genetically matched to a patient. Regenerating tissue in this way would avoid immune rejection.

[3] The public's response to this embryonic stem cell cloning technique is mixed. Yet perhaps surprisingly, 59% of those surveyed agreed with controversial research, according to figures released by the International Council on Medicine (ICM). The slight majority of respondents, 51% supported genetic engineering when used to correct physical defects in the fetus. This demonstrates that public attitudes toward genetic engineering have undergone a positive change, and it also bodes well for scientists who assert that cloning is the best way to find cures for some of society's most serious genetic disorders.

[4] Although the majority of the public condones the use of genetic engineering to cure illness or assist with organ transplants, many still resist the idea of parents creating "designer babies." The ICM survey results revealed that only 13% of respondents were in support of the parents using genetic engineering to "design" an unborn child, with 63% opposing such use. A marginally higher result, 20% of 18- to 24-year-olds said they would support the practice, which implies that future generations may be more open-minded about the idea.

[5] Currently, it is only legally possible to carry out two kinds of reproductive assistance on humans using In Vitro Fertilization to fertilize eggs outside the mother's body. The first procedure involves determining the genes and sex of the unborn baby. The second technique, called Pre-implantation Genetic Diagnosis, conducts embryo screening for genetic diseases, with only selected embryos implanted into the mother's womb. In the future, we may be able to use what is called germ line therapy to "cure" genetic diseases in embryos by substituting healthy DNA for faulty sections of DNA. Such therapy has been carried out on animal embryos successfully, but it is currently illegal to do this procedure on human embryos.

[6] Fears are that cloning techniques will be taken even further and used to screen personality traits in the unborn child, from their hair or eye color to their ability to perform well in sports or exams. While it may be years before public opinion truly supports us "designing" unborn children, scientists have the public's go-ahead to continue utilizing genetic engineering to help us all live healthier, longer lives.

[7] The advancement of genetic engineering has also been supported by the recent human genome project. Scientists and their publicists have used words and phrases such as "renaissance," "holy grail," and "the book of life" to describe this project, which they see as having huge benefits for health care worldwide. Nevertheless, like the new cloning technique described above, the human genome project also has its critics. Its detractors, like myself, insist that its defining feature is simply its large size. Furthermore, this worship of size is a fitting signifier for science in an era of globalization and multinational corporations. However, it is a better understanding of organisms, and therefore of disease, which other people see as the true promise of the human genome.

[8] Researchers are also currently gathering public opinion on human egg donation, which seeks views on whether scientists should be permitted to seek voluntary donations of human eggs for research purposes. Their research suggests that this might not be as controversial as it once seemed, because of the benefits of conducting research into using newly-created tissue to treat disease. This means that transplant patients would no longer be required to wait for another human's donor tissue that their bodies could reject. They could have themselves cloned instead to produce perfectly-matched tissue.

[9] We are promised genetic tests that will tell us whether we are susceptible to heart disease or cancer. Yet, what will we do with this information? And do we even want it? There is evidence that most people who may be at risk from Huntington's disease, which kills in middle age and for which there is no cure, do not want to know if they have the gene. Even if we can change our lifestyles, will we do so? Many people may treat susceptibility-prediction as inevitability and relapse into even worse lifestyles. Only one thing seems certain: the designing of new treatments targeted at genes involved in disease will be massively complicated because of the involvement of many different genes.

11. Which of these is most likely the author's purpose for writing this article?
    A. The author wants the reader to understand how stem cell cloning has changed over time.
    B. The author wants the reader to understand that genetic engineering can be used to cure illnesses.
    C. The author wants the reader to understand that there are debates surrounding genetic engineering.
    D. The author wants the reader to understand how researchers are assessing public opinion on using newly-created tissue to treat disease.

12. **Part A**
    How does the author provide effective support for the main idea of the article?
    A. The author describes new developments in the cloning of mice.
    B. The author summarizes various public views on genetic engineering.
    C. The author explains information about the human genome project.
    D. The author explains that several genetic procedures are controversial.

13. **Part B**
    Which detail from the article best supports the answer to Part A?
    A. Although the majority of the public condones the use of genetic engineering to cure illness or assist with organ transplants, many still resist the idea of parents creating "designer babies."
    B. Currently, it is only legally possible to carry out two kinds of reproductive assistance on humans using In Vitro Fertilization to fertilize eggs outside the mother's body.
    C. While it may be years before public opinion truly supports us "designing" unborn children, scientists have the public's go-ahead to continue utilizing genetic engineering to help us all live healthier, longer lives.
    D. Such therapy has been carried out on animal embryos successfully, but it is currently illegal to do this procedure on human embryos.

14. **Part A**
    Which statement explains how paragraph 2 develops the author's claim about the benefits of generating early-stage embryos?
    A. The paragraph explains that they can be used as tissue transplants.
    B. The paragraph explains that they will help in the process of legalizing cloning.
    C. The paragraph explains that they are very compact in size.
    D. The paragraph explains that they will help reduce tissue rejection.

15. **Part B**
    Which sentence from the article best supports the answer to part A?
    A. In the long term, scientists want to use such legalized cloning to generate therapies.
    B. A patient's skin cell could generate a cloned embryo which is grown for just a few days, at which point it is the size of a pin head.
    C. Regenerating tissue in this way would avoid immune rejection.
    D. The public's response to this embryonic stem cell cloning technique is mixed.

16. **Part A**
    Which statement represents a claim made by the author in paragraph 6?
    A. Most people disagree with "designer babies."
    B. Some people are afraid that the new cloning techniques will be used inappropriately.
    C. New cloning techniques could be used to make us live longer.
    D. New cloning techniques could be used to screen an unborn child for genetic diseases.

17. **Part B**
    Which detail from the article best supports the answer to Part A?
    A. The public's response to this embryonic stem cell cloning technique is mixed.
    B. Although the majority of the public condones the use of genetic engineering to cure illness or assist with organ transplants, many still resist the idea of parents creating "designer babies."
    C. Fears are that cloning techniques will be taken even further and used to screen personality traits in the unborn child, from their hair or eye color to their ability to perform well in sports or exams
    D. There is evidence that most people who may be at risk from Huntington's disease, which kills in middle age and for which there is no cure, do not want to know if they have the gene.

18. **Part A**
    Which statement represents a criticism made by the author in paragraph 7?
    A. The human genome project is not available worldwide.
    B. The only unique aspect of the human genome project is that it is a big project.
    C. The human genome project will only help multinational corporations.
    D. The human genome project will be impeded by advancing globalization.

19. **Part B**
    Which sentence from the article best supports the answer to Part A?
    A. Scientists and their publicists have used words and phrases such as "renaissance," "holy grail," and "the book of life" to describe this project, which they see as having huge benefits for health care worldwide.
    B. Nevertheless, like the new cloning technique described above, the human genome project also has its critics.
    C. Its detractors, like myself, insist that its defining feature is simply its large size.
    D. However, it is a better understanding of organisms, and therefore of disease, which other people see as the true promise of the human genome.

20. The author suggests that which of the following potential negative outcomes could occur when a person receives the results of a genetic test?
    A. People with incurable illnesses may stop taking care of themselves.
    B. They may not be able to get the drugs they need.
    C. They may not allow their information to be used for research purposes.
    D. People will not be allowed to take the test voluntarily.

[1] What's the difference between teaching engineering and economics? Is explicating concepts and facts to others the same procedure, regardless of the discipline? Absolutely not, says Amelia Emerson, who teaches older adults painting and decorating skills. "When I did my education degree at college, I felt it was more for academic teachers than vocational teachers like me," she says. "For me, I felt it wasn't useful."

[2] The Edge Foundation is a U.K. charity receiving governmental support in order to aid in practical and vocational learning and has agreed to fund the development and approval of new courses. The first 30 teacher trainees are to commence work later this month. Unlike previous teachers in training, these student-teachers, who want to teach vocational subjects like construction and photography, will not have to waste time by composing essays on pedagogy, says Joseph Smith, the college's president. When the students get together, they will be sharing their teaching techniques with each another. For the majority of the time they will actually be teaching, says Smith. "Teacher training should be work-based learning. Students in vocations are not going to learn by sitting in classrooms."

[3] Gary Martin, 37, is one of the new teachers participating in the Edge Foundation's program. After more than a decade working as a carpenter, he is now learning how to teach. "I have taught a few apprentices on site, and I really enjoyed doing it. Nobody's born knowing how to use tools. We all have to learn in a hands-on way," he says.

[4] "Historically, the view of official governing bodies has always been that teachers should have academic degrees," says Martin. However, in the past ten years or so, vocational teaching has come under the spotlight. He explains that "employers of teachers were telling us that while we were enhancing their academic skills, what was really needed was teachers who were better at teaching." Emphasizing that the new courses will focus entirely on subject-specific teaching skills, Martin said: "Trainees were getting a very solid foundation in teaching skills in general, but they were not getting sufficient teaching in their subject areas." To rectify that shortcoming, each trainee on the new course will work with a mentor who teaches in their subject area. They will submit videos of themselves teaching, rather than formal essays, and they will receive special cameras to record their own lessons.

[5] In addition to these reforms, new programs are also underway to improve the educational system itself. The U.K. government has earmarked funds for the Excellence in Education project, which was introduced at various colleges yesterday. The project celebrates achievement in colleges and champions the work taking place under the leadership of gifted professionals.

[6] Yet, across the world, it is a challenge to raise educational standards for everyone. In Chicago, for instance, results for ethnic minority children are rising faster than the average. Thus, what is needed is a far more plural system. So, if a college can attract students and meet basic standards, it should be able to receive governmental funding and students should have the right to find their places.

[7] In addition, U.S. researchers assert that we need a rigorous concentration on academic standards. The government was right to address this problem in educational reforms last year, but we need to go further. We should also reform the exam system to ensure that there is no devaluation of academic standards and college graduates have the skills required for a more competitive job market.

[8] Besides reforming student-teaching programs and improving academic standards, the physical premises where education takes place, namely college and school buildings, need to be considered. An influential pressure group has questioned the value of the government's $45 billion program to replace or refurbish all high schools and colleges over the next 15 years. Governmental officials will suggest that some of the cash might be better directed to making buildings more environmentally sustainable, reducing carbon emissions, or boosting pre-school learning. An increase in university research budgets should also be considered, they suggest.

[9] Again, we may be able to look to the British system for insight. The report on the U.K.'s Building Schools for the Future (BSF) program does not say the program is a waste of money nor recommend that it be stopped, but says the scheme must be regularly reviewed. Many governmental officials also want local authorities to have more freedom over the regeneration of schools and colleges. There have been complaints that the government may force them into becoming private academies as part of BSF.

[10] U.S. Governmental officials have asked whether $45 billion was too much to be spent on the buildings. One official stated: "BSF has begun by providing resources to areas with low levels of educational attainment. Once those areas have their projects in place, it could be argued that investment to replace buildings becomes less of a priority. That might be the point at which BSF and similar programs could be drawn to a close and a different approach to capital and other investment in schools could be adopted."

21. **Part A**
    What is the main purpose of paragraphs 1 to 4 of this article?
    A. To describe new educational reforms in general
    B. To summarize the views of teachers to a new education policy
    C. To provide details about a new teacher training program
    D. To point out current controversies in educational reform

22. **Part B**
    Which detail from the article best supports the answer to Part A?
    A. This and similar complaints are why U.S. educational reformers are looking into a new British project that is underway to assist colleges that train students to teach vocational subjects.
    B. The Edge Foundation is a U.K. charity receiving governmental support in order to aid in practical and vocational learning and has agreed to fund the development and approval of new courses.
    C. Gary Martin, 37, is one of the new teachers participating in the Edge Foundation's program.
    D. Historically, the view of official governing bodies has always been that teachers should have academic degrees.

23. Why does the author mention minority children from Chicago in paragraph 6?
    A. To demonstrate the difficulty of raising educational standards
    B. To argue for a more diverse educational system
    C. To show that schools need funding more than students
    D. To illustrate the needs of minority children

24. **Part A**
    According to the author, what two reforms of the examination system are currently necessary?
    A. Ensuring that new teachers have the necessary skills
    B. Maintaining fairness to minority students
    C. Increasing the plurality and diversity of the system
    D. Making sure exams are not devalued
    E. Protecting and maintaining academic standards
    F. Providing more funding for exams

25. **Part B**
    What sentence from the article best supports the answer to Part A?
    A. We should also reform the exam system to ensure that there is no devaluation of academic standards and college graduates have the skills required for a more competitive job market.
    B. Thus, what is needed is a far more plural system.

C. So, if a college can attract students and meet basic standards, it should be able to receive governmental funding and students should have the right to find their places.
D. Besides reforming student-teaching programs and improving academic standards, the physical premises where education takes place, namely college and school buildings, need to be considered.

26. **Part A**
According to the author, what question surrounds the $45 billion program to reform existing school buildings?
A. Whether the buildings should be replaced or refurbished
B. Whether the buildings should be environmentally friendly
C. What the money should actually be spent on
D. What the best upgrade of research facilities would be

27. **Part B**
What sentence from the article best supports the answer to Part A?
A. Besides reforming student-teaching programs and improving academic standards, the physical premises where education takes place, namely college and school buildings, need to be considered.
B. An influential pressure group has questioned the value of the government's $45 billion program to replace or refurbish all high schools and colleges over the next 15 years.
C. Governmental officials will suggest that some of the cash might be better directed to making buildings more environmentally sustainable, reducing carbon emissions, or boosting pre-school learning.
D. U.S. Governmental officials have asked whether $45 billion was too much to be spent on the buildings.

28. According to the article, what does the report on the Building Schools for the Future (BSF) recommend?
A. The program should be terminated.
B. The program should be monitored on a regular basis.
C. The program should utilize more private companies.
D. The program should receive more funding.

29. **Part A**
What criticism of the Building Schools for the Future (BSF) program do local authorities have?
A. They have become less of a priority.
B. A different approach should be adopted.
C. They think too much money has been spent.
D. They may be required to become academies.

30. **Part B**
What sentence from the article best supports the answer to Part A?
A. Many governmental officials also want local authorities to have more freedom over the regeneration of schools and colleges.
B. There have been complaints that the government may force them into becoming private academies as part of BSF.
C. BSF has begun by providing resources to areas with low levels of educational attainment. Once those areas have their projects in place, it could be argued that investment to replace buildings becomes less of a priority.
D. That might be the point at which BSF and similar programs could be drawn to a close and a different approach to capital and other investment in schools could be adopted.

Everyone knows that the insurance industry is continually raising monthly premiums, and many feel this is unjust to consumers. However, many people do not realize that the insurance industry has had to fight increasing insurance fraud. The amount of money spent on investigating and prosecuting fraud is then passed on to policyholders.

In spite of its prevalence, many people do not understand what insurance fraud entails. With reports estimating insurance fraud costs $30 billion to over $100 billion per year, the topic should not be taken lightly. Every insurance policyholder should understand what insurance fraud is and know its consequences. In this way, consumers will not only be more able to recognize and fight fraud, but will also be able to help reduce the cost that fraud causes insurance companies to suffer.

Insurance fraud is defined as intentionally deceiving, misrepresenting, or concealing information to receive benefits from one's insurance company. Importantly, insurance fraud includes even a **small fiddle**. Essentially fraud is committed any time a policyholder asserts that he or she has suffered a theft or other loss which was not actually suffered and is submitting a claim to the insurance company to receive reimbursement.

Another type of fraud is to experience an actual loss, but overstating the value of that loss. For example, a policyholder might own a $500 computer which was stolen, but will claim that the value of the computer was $1,000. Policyholders often attempt to justify their behavior by making a false claim for what they believe to be an insignificant amount, thinking that their claim is small in comparison to the massive revenue that the insurance company is making.

Perpetrators of insurance fraud also feel vindicated because of the knowledge that they have paid premiums for a certain number of years, so they believe that they deserve something back from the insurance company. But fraudulent claims are actually very pernicious for insurance companies and the insurance industry as a whole, and can result in fines and possible imprisonment.

Conversely, insurance fraud has developed recently that targets the policyholder more than the insurance company. Schemes have developed where fake insurance companies or agents sign unsuspecting customers for coverage at surprisingly low premium rates. They often act much like a regular insurance company for the first few months, but once there is a claim that needs to be reimbursed, the insurance company will disappear, along with the money paid in as premiums.

The rule with insurance fraud is much like that of any other scam: if a deal seems too good to be true, just remember that it probably is. Honesty is the best policy in dealings with insurance companies. Stay legal to avoid fines or prison and to continue receiving insurance coverage.

31. Which of these best explains the meaning of the phrase "a small fiddle"?
    A. a claim to the insurance company to receive reimbursement that is not substantial in amount
    B. intentionally deceiving, misrepresenting or concealing information
    C. experiencing an actual loss, but overstating the value of that loss
    D. making a false claim for what they believe to be an insignificant amount

32. **Part A**
    How does the author provide effective support for the main idea of the article?
    A. She argues that fraudulent insurance claims are a matter of conscience for the policymaker.
    B. She emphasizes the steps to combat the problem by insurance companies.
    C. She points out what fraudulent claims are by offering examples and explanations.
    D. She reveals that fraudulent claims may be much more prevalent than many people realize.

33. **Part B**
    Which detail from the article best supports the answer to Part A?
    A. Essentially fraud is committed any time a policyholder asserts that he or she has suffered a theft or other loss which was not actually suffered and is submitting a claim to the insurance company to receive reimbursement.
    B. Policyholders often attempt to justify their behavior by making a false claim for what they believe to be an insignificant amount, thinking that their claim is small in comparison to the massive revenue that the insurance company is making.
    C. But fraudulent claims are actually very pernicious for insurance companies and the insurance industry as a whole, and can result in fines and possible imprisonment.
    D. Conversely, insurance fraud has developed recently that targets the policyholder more than the insurance company.

34. **Part A**
    According to the author, why do some policyholders feel justified in making over-inflated claims?
    A. They think they are owed something in return because of what they have paid in.
    B. They think that everyone else is doing it, so they can too.
    C. They want to recover the loses they have incurred from fake insurance companies.
    D. They blame the insurance companies for not fighting fraud.

35. **Part B**
    Which detail from the article best supports the answer to Part A?
    A. In spite of its prevalence, many people do not understand what insurance fraud entails.
    B. With reports estimating insurance fraud costs $30 billion to over $100 billion per year, the topic should not be taken lightly.
    C. Perpetrators of insurance fraud also feel vindicated because of the knowledge that they have paid premiums for a certain number of years, so they believe that they deserve something back from the insurance company.
    D. Schemes have developed where fake insurance companies or agents sign unsuspecting customers for coverage at surprisingly low premium rates.

Many cities and towns are now thinking about computer recycling to protect the environment and avoid possible soil contamination. Because computers contain many parts that could release toxins into the soil, city governments are seeking alternative ways to dispose of antiquated computers, as well as all disused electronic equipment. This eventually will evolve into a normal practice as more municipalities become aware of the potential danger of dumping computers and other electronic products into landfills. Many activist groups are also spreading the word about computer recycling and want to find better ways to dispose of electronic equipment.

In many cities, there are local electronic shops or recycling centers that will take unwanted computers and other electronics, dismantle them, and place the parts into the correct respective containers for disposal. This method of disposal will soon become a necessity as the computer industry perpetually upgrades operating systems. In so doing, the industry effectively "enforces" a program whereby consumers have to replace old computers if they want to keep their equipment keep up-to-date. If obsolete computers continue to be placed into landfills as they have in the past, this situation will eventually cause environmental issues that may then need to be addressed by the government.

The average consumer does not appreciate that computer monitors and old-fashioned television sets contain gases and other toxins that leech into the soil if placed in landfill sites. It is an inevitability of nature that these gases will be released into the atmosphere as well. This is a concern for all who have the ozone and air quality in mind. Simply stated, the gases inside a monitor need to be released safely; without proper release, the ground and air will become filled with these toxic gases.

It is vital that everyone disposes of their computer equipment properly by taking it to a participating recycler in the area. A small fee will normally be charged for this service, but it is money wisely spent to protect the environment. Nevertheless, it is lamentable that some computer users will dispose of their unwanted equipment in a pile on the side of the road somewhere in order to avoid paying this small fee, rather than taking their equipment to a place that is accredited for safe disposal.

One of the issues surrounding computer disposal is the thousands if not millions of computers, printers, and monitors, as well as other electronics, that are already in landfills all over the world. Many people express concern about ways to clean up landfill sites that already have the electronics dumped there, but the cost would be in the millions to do such a huge project of this sort. Others argue that the electronics that have been in landfills for some time now should be left alone, having already done what harm they could do.

Printers just need the ink or toner cartridges removed before dismantling them. Many retail electronic outlets have barrels for disposing of empty printer cartridges, and some ink and toner manufactures even supply pre-paid envelopes for sending the old cartridges back for recycling. These practices have been around for quite a while now, and they have substantially reduced the quantity of cartridges being put in landfills.

Newer and improved computer systems are becoming readily available at affordable prices. In order to keep up with the relentless march of technological change, consumers are going to need new computers and other electronic equipment to meet the demands of our ever-changing world. More recycling centers are needed urgently since the quantity of disused computer equipment will double, if not triple, over the next few years.

Recycling old computers to save the environment is necessary and everyone has a responsibility to abide by this practice in order to protect and preserve land and air quality. The issue of recycling computers and other electronics has thus become a hot topic which the government should address in order to protect the environment for us and for future generations.

36. In the article, the writer makes no claim about which of the following?
    A. the provision of recycling by retail electronic stores
    B. the potential need for government involvement in resolving the issue of computer recycling
    C. the harm done by computers already in landfills
    D. the propensity of the average household to participate in local recycling schemes

37. **Part A**
    What claim does the author make in the article?
    A. Printers are relatively easy to dispose of.
    B. Recycling centers are widespread and easy to find.
    C. The computer industry itself causes people to get new computers.
    D. The gas inside a computer monitor is toxic.

38. **Part B**
    What detail from the passage best supports the answer to Part A?
    A. Many retail electronic outlets have barrels for disposing of empty printer cartridges.
    B. The industry effectively "enforces" a program whereby consumers have to replace old computers if they want to keep their equipment up-to-date.
    C. Simply stated, the gases inside a monitor need to be released safely.
    D. Without proper release, the ground and air will become filled with these toxic gases.

39. Which of the following sentences does not provide a logical step in the structure of the writer's argument?
    A. In many cities, there are local electronic shops or recycling centers that will take unwanted computers and other electronics, dismantle them, and place the parts into the correct respective containers for disposal.
    B. The issue of recycling computers and other electronics has thus become a hot topic which the government should address in order to protect the environment for us and for future generations.
    C. It is vital that everyone disposes of their computer equipment properly by taking it to a participating recycler in the area.
    D. Printers just need the ink or toner cartridges removed before dismantling them.

40. Which statement below best states the main cause of environmental damage from computer disposal today?
    A. Toxic gases from computers that are not disposed of properly are being released into the earth and atmosphere.
    B. There is insufficient involvement of groups and organizations to raise awareness about computer recycling.
    C. Some computer users dispose of their unwanted equipment in a pile on the side of the road.
    D. There is a certain amount of apathy about ways to clean up landfill sites that already have computer equipment dumped in them.

English Language Skills Section

Grammar Guide

The sections in the following part of the study guide are intended as an overview of the aspects of grammar most commonly tested on the exam. Read each section carefully, paying special attention to the examples. Then take the practice writing tests that follow.

Adverb Placement

Adverbs are words that express how an action was done. Adverbs often end in the suffix –ly. You can vary adverb placement, depending upon what you want to emphasize in your sentence. Be sure to place the adverb in the correct position in the sentence and to use the comma, if necessary. If the adverb is used as the first word in a sentence, the adverb should be followed by a comma.

> CORRECT: Normally, an economic crisis is a valid reason to raise interest rates.
>
> CORRECT: An economic crisis is normally a valid reason to raise interest rates.
>
> INCORRECT: An economic crisis is a valid reason to normally raise interest rates.

Remember not to place an adverb between "to" and the verb, as in the last example above. This practice, known as the split infinitive, is grammatically incorrect.

Commonly-Confused Words

Be careful with the following commonly-confused words:

- adverse (adjective – detrimental) / averse (adjective – reluctant)
- affect (verb – to cause) / effect (noun – the result or outcome)
- allude (imply) / elude (evade)
- allusion (implication) / illusion (appearance)
- bare (verb – to expose) / bear (verb – to take on a burden)
- bale (noun – a cubed package) / bail (verb – to get something out of something else)
- pore (verb – to study or read with care) / pour (verb – to emit or flow)
- principal (adjective – main or predominant)/ principle (noun – a concept)

Now look at the following examples.

> CORRECT: Failure to study will <u>affect</u> your grades.
>
> INCORRECT: Failure to study will <u>effect</u> your grades.
>
> CORRECT: A scientific <u>principle</u> is a concise statement about the relationship of one object to another.
>
> INCORRECT: A scientific <u>principal</u> is a concise statement about the relationship of one object to another.
>
> CORRECT: The run-away thief <u>eluded</u> the police officer.
>
> INCORRECT: The run-away thief <u>alluded</u> the police officer.

CORRECT: He thought he saw an oasis in the desert, but it was an optical illusion.

INCORRECT: He thought he saw an oasis in the desert, but it was an optical allusion.

CORRECT: I was depending on her help, but she bailed out at the last minute.

INCORRECT: I was depending on her help, but she baled out at the last minute.

CORRECT: He pored over the book as he studied for the exam.

INCORRECT: He poured over the book as he studied for the exam.

CORRECT: She is averse to receiving help with the project.

INCORRECT: She is adverse to receiving help with the project.

CORRECT: He could not bear to listen to the loud music.

INCORRECT: He could not bare to listen to the loud music.

Misplaced Modifiers

Modifiers are descriptive phrases. The modifier should always be placed directly before or after the noun to which it relates. Now look at the examples.

CORRECT: Like Montana, Wyoming is not very densely populated.

INCORRECT: Like Montana, there isn't a large population in Wyoming.

The phrase "like Montana" is an adjectival phrase that describes or modifies the noun "Wyoming." Therefore, "Wyoming" must come directly after the comma.

Here are two more examples:

CORRECT: While waiting at the bus stop, a senior citizen was mugged.

INCORRECT: While waiting at the bus stop, a mugging took place.

The adverbial phrase "while waiting at the bus stop" modifies the noun phrase "a senior citizen," so this noun phrase needs to come after the adverbial phrase.

Parallel Structure

Correct parallel structure is also known as parallelism. In order to follow the grammatical rules of parallelism, you must be sure that all of the items you give in a series are of the same part of speech. So, all of the items must be nouns or verbs, for example. In other words, you should not use both nouns and verbs in a list. Where verbs are used, they should be in the same form or tense.

CORRECT: The vacation gave me a great chance to unwind, have fun, and experience some excitement. (*Unwind*, *have*, and *experience* are all verbs.)

INCORRECT: The vacation gave me a great chance to unwind, and was fun and quite exciting.

CORRECT: I went jet-skiing, surfing, and snorkeling on our vacation. (*Skiing, surfing,* and *snorkeling* are all in the –ing form.)

INCORRECT: I went jet-skiing, surfing, and also snorkeled on our vacation.

CORRECT: The hotel was elegant, comfortable, and modern. (*Elegant, comfortable,* and *modern* are all adjectives.)

INCORRECT: The hotel was elegant, comfortable, and had up-to-date facilities.

CORRECT: I enjoyed our hotel room, relaxed in the spa, and ate some truly delicious food on our vacation. (*Enjoyed, relaxed,* and *ate* are all verbs in the past simple tense.)

INCORRECT: I enjoyed our hotel room, relaxed in the spa, and the food was truly delicious on our vacation.

Pronoun-Antecedent Agreement

Pronouns are words like the following: he, she, it, they, and them. An antecedent is a phrase that precedes the pronoun in the sentence. Pronouns must agree with their antecedents, so use singular pronouns with singular antecedents and plural pronouns with plural antecedents. Be careful not to mix singular and plural forms.

CORRECT: Each student needs to bring his or her identification to the placement test.

INCORRECT: Each student needs to bring their identification to the placement test.

The antecedent "each student" is singular, so the singular pronouns "his" or "her" should follow this antecedent.

CORRECT: The group lost its enthusiasm for the project.

INCORRECT: The group lost their enthusiasm for the project.

The preceding sentence is incorrect because the antecedent is "group," which is singular, while "their" is plural.

Pronoun Usage – Correct Use of *Its* and *It's*

"Its" is a possessive pronoun, while "it's" is a contraction of "it is".

CORRECT: It's high time you started to study.

INCORRECT: Its high time you started to study.

The sentence could also be stated as follows: It is high time you started to study.

Since the contracted form of "it is" can be used in the alternative sentence above, "it's" is the correct form.

CORRECT: A snake sheds its skin at least once a year.

INCORRECT: A snake sheds it's skin at least once a year.

"Its" is a possessive pronoun referring to the snake, so the apostrophe should not be used.

Pronoun Usage – Demonstrative Pronouns

Demonstrative pronouns include the following words: this, that, these, those

"This" is used for a singular item that is nearby. "That" is used for singular items that are farther away in time or space.

> SINGULAR: This book that I have here is really interesting.
>
> PLURAL: That book on the table over there is really interesting.

"These" is used for plural items that are nearby. "Those" is used for plural items that are farther away in time or space.

> SINGULAR: These pictures in my purse were taken on our vacation.
>
> PLURAL: Those pictures on the wall were taken on our vacation.

Avoid using "them" instead of "those":

> INCORRECT: Them pictures on the wall were taken on our vacation.

Pronoun Usage – Relative Pronouns

Relative pronouns include the following: which, that, who, whom, whose

"Which" and "that" are used to describe things, and "who" and "whom" are used to describe people. "Whose" is used for people or things.

> WHICH: Last night, I watched a romantic-comedy movie which was really funny.
>
> THAT: Last night, I watched a romantic-comedy movie that was really funny.
>
> WHO: Susan always remains calm under pressure, unlike Tom, who is always so nervous.

"Who" is used because we are describing the person. This is known as the nominative case.

> WHOM: To whom should the report be given?

"Whom" is used because the person is receiving an action, which in this case is receiving the report. This is known as the accusative case.

> WHOSE: I went out for lunch with Marta, whose parents are from Costa Rica.
>
> WHOSE: I went out for lunch yesterday at that new restaurant, whose name I don't remember.

Please be sure to look at the section entitled "Restrictive and Non-restrictive Modifiers" for information on how to use punctuation with relative pronouns.

Proper Nouns and Proper Adjectives – Capitalization

Proper nouns state the names of specific people, places, ideas, or things. The names of people, countries, states, buildings, streets, rivers, oceans, countries, companies, and institutions are proper nouns. Be careful not to confuse common nouns and proper nouns. Proper adjectives are derived from proper nouns, so they refer to unique classes of people, places, or things. Proper nouns and adjectives should be capitalized. Look at the capitalization in the following examples.

> CORRECT: A famous American landmark, the geyser named Old Faithful is located in Yellowstone Park in the northwest corner of the state of Wyoming. (*American* is a proper adjective. *Old Faithful*, *Yellowstone Park*, and *Wyoming* are proper nouns.)

> INCORRECT: A famous american landmark, the geyser named old faithful is located in yellowstone park in the Northwest corner of the State of wyoming.

Punctuation – Using the Apostrophe for Possessive Forms

Apostrophe placement depends upon whether a word is singular or plural.

For the singular, the apostrophe should be placed before the letter "s."

> SINGULAR: Our team's performance was poor at the game last night.

For the plural form, the apostrophe should be placed after the letter "s."

> PLURAL: Both teams' performances were poor at the game last night.

Remember that the apostrophe is used in sentences like those above in order to show possession. Also remember not to use the apostrophe unnecessarily.

> INCORRECT: The date's for the events are June 22 and July 5.

> INCORRECT: The dates' for the events are June 22 and July 5.

Punctuation – Using Colons and Semicolons

Colons (:) should be used when giving a list of items. Semicolons (;) should be used to join independent clauses.

> COLON: The shop is offering discounts on the following items: DVDs, books, and magazines.

> SEMICOLON: I thought I would live in this city forever; then I lost my job.

Note that the word following the semicolon should not be capitalized.

Please see the section entitled "Punctuation and Independent Clauses" for more information on joining clauses.

Punctuation – Using Commas with Dates and Locations

Commas should be used after the date and year in dates. Commas should also be used after towns and states.

DATES: On July 4, 1776, the Declaration of Independence was signed.

LOCATIONS: Located in Seattle, Washington, the Space Needle is a major landmark.

Punctuation – Using Commas for Items in a Series

When using "and" and "or" for more than two items in a series, be sure to use the comma before the words "and" and "or."

CORRECT: You need to bring a tent, sleeping bag, and flashlight.

INCORRECT: You need to bring a tent, sleeping bag and flashlight.

Notice the use of the comma after the word "bag" and before the word "and" in the series.

CORRECT: Students can call, write a letter, or send an email.

INCORRECT: Students can call, write a letter or send an email.

Notice the use of the comma after the word "letter" and before the word "or" in the series.

Punctuation and Independent Clauses – Avoiding Run-On Sentences

Run-on sentences are those that use commas to join independent clauses together, instead of correctly using the period.

Because they incorrectly use the comma to fuse sentences together, run-on sentences are sometimes called comma splices.

An independent clause contains a grammatical subject and verb. It therefore can stand alone as its own sentence.

The first word of the independent clause should begin with a capital letter, and the clause should be preceded by a period.

CORRECT: I thought I would live in this city forever. Then I lost my job.

INCORRECT: I thought I would live in this city forever, then I lost my job.

"Then I lost my job" is a complete sentence. It has a grammatical subject (I) and a verb (lost).

The independent clause must be preceded by a period, and the first word of the new sentence must begin with a capital letter.

Alternatively, an appropriate conjunction can be used to join the independent clauses:

CORRECT: I thought I would live in this city forever, and then I lost my job.

Restrictive and Non-restrictive Modifiers

Restrictive modifiers are clauses or phrases that provide essential information in order to identify the grammatical subject. Restrictive modifiers should not be preceded by a comma.

CORRECT: My sister who lives in Indianapolis is a good swimmer. (The speaker has more than one sister.)

In this case, the speaker has more than one sister, and she is identifying which sister she is talking about by giving the essential information "who lives in Indianapolis."

On the other hand, a non-restrictive modifier is a clause or phrase that provides extra information about a grammatical subject in a sentence. A non-restrictive modifier must be preceded by a comma. Non-restrictive modifiers are also known as non-essential modifiers.

CORRECT: My sister, who lives in Indianapolis, is a good swimmer. (The speaker has only one sister.)

In this case, the speaker has only one sister. Therefore, the information about her sister's city of residence is not essential in order to identify which sister she is talking about. The words "who lives in Indianapolis" form a non-restrictive modifier.

Sentence Fragments

A sentence fragment is a group of words that does not express a complete train of thought.

CORRECT: I like Denver because it has a great university.

INCORRECT: I like Denver. Because it has a great university.

In the second example, "because it has a great university" is not a complete thought. This idea needs to be joined with the previous clause in order to be grammatically correct.

Subject-Verb Agreement

For questions on subject-verb agreement, you need to be sure that subjects agree with verbs in number. In other words, use a singular verb with a singular subject and a plural verb with a plural subject. While this sounds straightforward, complications can arise with certain words like "each," "every," "neither," and "either," all of which are in fact singular. Subject-verb agreement can also be confusing when there are intervening words in a sentence.

CORRECT: The flowers in the pots in the garden grow quickly.

INCORRECT: The flowers in the pots in the garden grows quickly.

The grammatical subject in the above sentence is "flowers," not "garden," so the plural form of the verb (*grow*) needs to be used.

CORRECT: Each person in the groups of students needs to pay attention to the instructions.

INCORRECT: Each person in the groups of students need to pay attention to the instructions.

The grammatical subject in the above sentence is "each person," not "students." "Each" is singular and therefore requires the singular form of the verb (*needs*).

CORRECT: Each of the men is very strong and determined.

INCORRECT: Every one of the books are on the shelf.

Subordination

Subordinators include words and phrases such as "although," "but," "even though," "because of," and "due to." Be careful to use commas correctly when subordinating sentences.

CORRECT: I was going to study this evening, but the noise next door made it impossible.

INCORRECT: I was going to study this evening but the noise next door made it impossible.

CORRECT: Although I was going to study this evening, the noise next door made it impossible.

INCORRECT: Although I was going to study this evening the noise next door made it impossible.

The word "but" is a subordinator. Subordinators need to be preceded by a comma, so the first sentence is correct as written.

You also need to use a comma in the middle of the sentence when beginning the sentence with the subordinator.

Review of Verb Tenses:

Present simple tense

The present simple tense is used for habitual actions.

>Example: He *goes* to the office at 8:00 every morning.

The present tense is also used to state scientific truths, facts, and generalizations.

>Example: Water *freezes* at zero degrees Celsius.

Past simple tense

The past simple tense is used for actions that were started and completed in the past.

>Example: I walked three miles yesterday.

Present perfect tense

The present perfect tense is used for actions that were completed in the past, but that have relevancy in the present time.

>Example: I *have studied* every day this week.

The phrase "this week" shows that the action has relevancy in the present time.

Past perfect tense

The past perfect tense is used for an action that was completed in the past, prior to another action that was completed in the past.

>Example: We had just sent the letter when the email arrived.

Passive tenses

Use the passive voice to emphasize the object of the action, rather than the person who was conducting the action.

In the example sentence that follows in this section, the diplomas are the object of the action.

We want to emphasize the fact that students are receiving the diplomas. We want to de-emphasize the fact that the university officials are the people responsible for handing out the diplomas.

> Example: Diplomas *are handed out* on graduation day every year.

The passive can also take more complicated forms.

> Example: Ronald Reagan was the only former actor *to have been elected* President in the twentieth century.

The general populace of the United States elects the president. We want to emphasize who was elected, rather than who did the electing, so we need to use the perfect form of the passive in the preceding sentence.

Source, Reference, and Citation Guide

Sources

You will need to know about citation and referencing during your time at college, and your exam may have one or two questions in this area.

<u>Primary sources</u> – original information in the form of a text, document, manuscript, survey, or statistical data.

Examples: Archives at the county court house on births and deaths

  Records held by an institution

  A literary manuscript produced by the author

<u>Secondary sources</u> – commentary, discussion, or analysis of the primary source.

Examples: An independent research report analyzing births and deaths in the county

  A newspaper article that comments on the records held by the institution

  An article in a scholarly journal that discusses the literary manuscript

Use of sources

Be sure that you know how to use lists of references in your own research. You may encounter an exam question on this research technique.

When you are conducting research for a dissertation, term paper, or report, you should pay special attention to the list of references cited at the end of the book or article.

You can read the sources provided in the list of references, and then identify and note down the names of interesting-looking books and articles that the author has cited. You can then read these sources later and cite them in your own research.

Referencing

You should be able to identify what type of source is being referenced when you look at a citation. Note that citations vary in format, depending on what type of material is being used. Study the following citations and notice the slight differences in format for each one.

Books:

Brown, Mark. (2020). *Old towns: A study in urban development.* Pittsburg: Authors' Press.

Notice that only the year is given for a book. Also note that the title is given in italic font. The place and company of publication are provided at the end of a book citation.

Academic or Scholarly Journal:

Tauton, Rachel. (2019). The use of audio in the English classroom. *Pedagogy and Learning, 23*(4), 13-21.

Notice that the volume and issue numbers [*23*(4)] are provided for a scholarly journal. In addition, the page numbers are given at the end of the citation in the following format: 13-21. The name of the journal is given in italics, but the title of the article is not italicized.

Magazines:

Haas, Assan. (2018, May 9). Power in the new millennium. *Popular Technology, 135*, 28-31.

Notice that the date for a magazine citation is in the following format: (2018, May 9). The issue number will be given (*135*), followed by the page numbers (28-31). The name of the magazine is given in italics, but the title of the article is not italicized.

Newspapers:

Gomez, Joaquin. (2015, January 28). The cost to the taxpayer of state energy policies. *The News Today*, pp. 2B, 3A.

The date for a newspaper citation is in the same format as that of a magazine: (2018 May 9). However, the page numbers for a newspaper state the section and page number in this format: pp. 2B, 3A. The name of the newspaper is given in italics, but the title of the article is not italicized.

Online sources:

Papadopoulos, Maria. (2012). Twenty top study tips. *Lists for Busy People.* Retrieved from https://www.alistapart.com/articles/lists

A URL or web address needs to be provided for citations of online materials. The name of the website is given in italics, but the title of the article is not italicized.

GRAMMAR AND USAGE EXERCISES – SET 1

Instructions: Choose the word that best competes the sentence.

1. I don't know _____ the promotion or not. **(M)**
   A. whether got
   B. he got
   C. if he got
   D. that he got

2. Bob is upset because he saw a bad accident that _____ this morning. **(E)**
   A. was happening
   B. happened
   C. has happening
   D. happen

3. Someone once advised me _____ to California in the summer. **(E)**
   A. not to go
   B. not going
   C. not go
   D. if I not go

4. _____ in reading popular novels. **(M)**
   A. I am interesting
   B. Interesting it is
   C. I am interested
   D. It is interesting

5. That device is a machine _____ digital data. **(M)**
   A. by which encoded
   B. which are encoded
   C. by which are encoded
   D. which encodes

6. _____ her only once since she went away to college. **(E)**
   A. I have seen
   B. Did I seen
   C. Have I seen
   D. I see

7. The last few months _____ their toll on him. **(E)**
   A. taken
   B. have taken
   C. made
   D. have made

8. You would have passed your test _____ more. **(M)**
   A. had you studied
   B. if you studied
   C. you had studied
   D. would you studied

9. That restaurant has dishes that aren't _____ anywhere else. **(E)**
   A. to be served
   B. serving
   C. served
   D. to serve

10. _____ it, I can't really say if I like skiing. **(E)**
    A. Never having tried
    B. Never had trying
    C. Never to have tried
    D. Never to try

11. She would have _____ in the accident had she not put on her seat belt. **(E)**
    A. injury
    B. been injuring
    C. been injured
    D. to be injured

12. To _____ a long story short, I decided not to go to Los Angeles. **(E)**
    A. take
    B. make
    C. taking
    D. making

13. People _____ about that new video. **(E)**
    A. constant talk
    B. constant talking
    C. constantly to be talking
    D. are constantly talking

14. He was evicted from his apartment, but what _____ was pay his rent on time. **(M)**
    A. he should do
    B. should he do
    C. he should have done
    D. he should be doing

15. The professor was telling us not _____ so much time talking. **(E)**
    A. spending
    B. to be spending
    C. to spending
    D. be spending

GRAMMAR AND USAGE EXERCISES – SET 2

1. We don't have any plans for tonight. How about _____ bowling? **(E)**
   A. to go
   B. we go
   C. going for
   D. going

2. Teachers get tired of students _____ about how much homework they are given. **(E)**
   A. to complain
   B. complaints

C. to have complained
D. complaining

3. If you want to go for a hamburger, I _____ one too. **(E)**
   A. like to have
   B. feel like to have
   C. feel like having
   D. feel like I have had

4. The new fitness center _____ next week. **(E)**
   A. be opening
   B. is being opening
   C. will opening
   D. is having its opening

5. Janet told me about the surprise party, although she _____ . **(E)**
   A. mightn't have
   B. won't have
   C. shouldn't have
   D. couldn't have

6. I have seen one of Grant Wood's paintings in a museum, but I _____ . **(M)**
   A. from where can't remember
   B. where can't remember
   C. can't remember from where
   D. can't remember where

7. I'm glad you _____ me that you had already completed the report. **(E)**
   A. had told
   B. told
   C. were telling
   D. tell

8. That presentation was far too advanced _____ as an introductory lecture. **(E)**
   A. to be suiting
   B. for suiting
   C. to be suitable
   D. suitably

9. He is _____ his three brothers. **(E)**
   A. taller of
   B. the tallest
   C. taller than
   D. tallest of

10. I really regret _____ harder to increase my savings. **(E)**
    A. not having tried
    B. not to try
    C. not to tried
    D. not to trying

11. He _____ me to repeat something four times yesterday. **(E)**
    A. had asked
    B. asked

C. has been asking
D. had been asking

12. We couldn't have completed the project without Ahmed, who _____ a great deal of expertise to the team. **(E)**
A. brought
B. had brought
C. will have brought
D. will be bringing

13. Once he _____ that he wasn't going to be able to go to college, he felt a lot better. **(M)**
A. accepts
B. did accept
C. will accept
D. had accepted

14. She was upset about not receiving an invitation; we _____ have invited her. **(E)**
A. must
B. may
C. should
D. ought

15. Your monetary compensation agreement is in the envelope _____ was forwarded to your attorney. **(E)**
A. which
B. in which
C. where
D. in that

GRAMMAR AND USAGE EXERCISES – SET 3

1. I expect her _____ out of her parents' house now that she has finished college. **(E)**
A. to move
B. moving
C. being moved
D. to have been moving

2. This isn't my first draft of the assignment; I _____ it. **(E)**
A. had yet re-written
B. re-wrote already
C. have already re-written
D. re-written already

3. He's getting married tomorrow, and _____ him so worried. **(M)**
A. never have I seen
B. never I saw
C. I have seen never
D. I never saw

4. Perhaps she _____ stay home than go shopping with us. **(E)**
A. might better
B. would rather
C. much better
D. could rather

5. He gets _____ grades of all the students in his class. **(E)**
   A. the best
   B. the better
   C. the best of
   D. better than

6. Just after we _____ , he decided to leave. **(M)**
   A. had arrived
   B. have arrived
   C. are arriving
   D. were arrived

7. The teacher told me off _____ to class. **(E)**
   A. to be late
   B. to being late
   C. for being late
   D. being late

8. I'm sure that _____ to Disneyland will be a lot of fun. **(E)**
   A. to go
   B. going
   C. to be going
   D. having gone

9. In addition to _____ , Susan also does knitting. **(E)**
   A. sew
   B. she sews
   C. sewing
   D. she sewing

10. My new job is going well now that I have gotten used _____ so early. **(E)**
    A. to getting up
    B. getting up
    C. to get up
    D. get up

11. _____ my best friend only once since she moved to Minneapolis. **(M)**
    A. I have seen
    B. Did I see
    C. Have I seen
    D. I saw

12. The doctor advised me to do something that I never would have thought _____. **(M)**
    A. to be done
    B. to do
    C. to doing
    D. of doing

13. It was time John _____ the situation. **(M)**
    A. accept
    B. accepted
    C. accepts
    D. was accepting

14. The new supermarket is believed _____ next week. **(M)**
    A. be closing
    B. to be closing
    C. it is closing
    D. to having its closing

15. That problem is between you and _____; you shouldn't discuss it with anyone else. **(D)**
    A. I
    B. me
    C. mine
    D. my

GRAMMAR AND USAGE EXERCISES – SET 4

1. I have no idea where I put my jacket. It could be _____. **(M)**
   A. anywhere
   B. elsewhere
   C. somewhere else
   D. other place

2. The remodeling on the upstairs of our house is _____ finished. **(M)**
   A. soon
   B. almost
   C. near
   D. far

3. Although he was extremely careful driving the car, he _____ an accident. **(M)**
   A. did
   B. has
   C. do have
   D. did have

4. You can put that bag on the seat between you and _____. **(D)**
   A. I
   B. me
   C. mine
   D. my

5. Many people like going for long walks in the park, but _____ do not. **(M)**
   A. another
   B. other
   C. others
   D. some other

6. That new student, _____ remember, is supposed to be very intelligent. **(M)**
   A. whose name I can't
   B. which name I can't
   C. that I can't name
   D. whom I can't name

7. There were many casualties in the area, even though the weather report said that _____ prepared for the tornado. **(M)**
   A. people should
   B. people should have

      C. people ought have
      D. ought people have

8. At 6'4" Jane is the _____ four sisters. **(M)**
      A. tallest of the
      B. taller of her
      C. taller than her
      D. most tall of the

9. Sarah told everyone my secret, but _____ we are still good friends. **(M)**
      A. furthermore
      B. despite of that
      C. contrarily
      D. in spite of that

10. I would have bought that new dress _____ more money. **(D)**
      A. did I have
      B. have I have
      C. if I did have
      D. had I had

11. I finally decided _____ New College after I got confirmation of my scholarship. **(E)**
      A. to attend
      B. to attend to
      C. attending
      D. to attend at

12. He got _____ cheating on the exam. **(E)**
      A. down with
      B. through with
      C. away with
      D. up to

13. We arrived at a solution that can _____ . **(M)**
      A. be achieved easy
      B. be easily achieved
      C. easy to be achieved
      D. easily to be achieved

14. He is so shy that not a word _____ during the meeting yesterday. **(D)**
      A. he did say
      B. was he saying
      C. did he say
      D. was it said

15. Our business is going quite well now that we have acquired all _____ we need to sell. **(E)**
      A. to the merchandise
      B. of the merchandise
      C. for the merchandise
      D. of merchandise

16. After the fire last week, the all of the paintings in the museum are believed _____ . **(D)**
      A. to have been destroyed
      B. destroyed

C. that are destroyed
D. to destroy

17. My grandma is coming to visit me _____ the beginning of the month. **(E)**
    A. in
    B. at
    C. on
    D within

18. If you hadn't eaten so much, you _____ a stomach ache. **(M)**
    A. might not have gotten
    B. ought not to have gotten
    C. might have gotten
    D. could get

19. _____ book is the best one I've read so far. **(E)**
    A. Those
    B. This
    C. Their's
    D. These

20. You're a fool if you believe her because she has told those lies and many _____ . **(E)**
    A. other
    B. another
    C. others
    D. anothers

GRAMMAR AND USAGE EXERCISES – SET 5

1. She is such a nervous person that very rarely _____ relaxed. **(D)**
    A. she appears
    B. she is appearing
    C. does she appear
    D. she does appear

2. The paper is in the cabinet _____ we use to store the pens and pencils. **(M)**
    A. that
    B. there
    C. where
    D. in which

3. Starting a new business involves sizing _____ the competition. **(E)**
    A. around
    B. under
    C. up
    D. over

4. We hope _____ on vacation on Saturday. **(E)**
    A. to go
    B. to going
    C. going
    D. to have been going

5.	No sooner _____ at the party than Sung Li came in. **(M)**
	A. we arrived
	B. we had arrived
	C. had we arrived
	D. we were arriving

6.	Alison is at home recovering _____ the flu. **(E)**
	A. with
	B. to
	C. for
	D. from

7.	She wouldn't have gotten fired _____ honest. **(M)**
	A. she was
	B. had she been
	C. was she
	D. she had been

8.	That was a pretty good movie, but I prefer the one _____ . **(M)**
	A. to which I saw last week
	B. I saw last week
	C. which last week I saw
	D. I saw it last week

9.	I requested that my friend _____ to the party. **(M)**
	A. to be invited
	B. be inviting
	C. to have been invited
	D. be invited

10.	Iced tea on a hot summer day is one of life's _____ pleasures. **(M)**
	A. greater
	B. most great
	C. greatest
	D. the greatest

11.	That form was compulsory, so _____ it in. **(E)**
	A. you should have filled
	B. should you have filled
	C. should have you filled
	D. you should filled

12.	I don't want to eat at McDonalds. I would rather eat _____ . **(E)**
	A. anyplace
	B. somewhere else
	C. somewhere
	D. other place

13.	_____ students here study a lot and work hard. **(E)**
	A. Almost
	B. Most of
	C. Almost of
	D. Most

14. The suspects were interrogated, but all of them denied _____ the car. **(E)**
    A. stealing
    B. to steal
    C. to stealing
    D. to have stolen

15. Although some people can't stand our boss, I can put _____ her sometimes. **(E)**
    A. down
    B. in for
    C. up with
    D. off

16. _____ my exam today, I wanted to get a good night's sleep last night. **(E)**
    A. While I have
    B. Because of
    C. While having
    D. Because having

17. She has many _____ hobbies apart from fitness and hiking. **(E)**
    A. other
    B. another
    C. others
    D. more of

18. I know you are normally very careful, but you _____ to be extra cautious when you travel. **(M)**
    A. did need
    B. do need
    C. have needed
    D. did

19. Although I will leave this job tomorrow, I feel so happy _____ with such wonderful people. **(M)**
    A. to have
    B. to have worked
    C. to have been worked
    D. worked

20. Even though the three of you have argued, _____ shouldn't have hard feelings against her. **(D)**
    A. you and he
    B. you and him
    C. him and you
    D. yours and his

SENTENCE FORMATION AND ESSAY DEVELOPMENT EXERCISES WITH TIPS

Instructions: Read the early drafts of the essays below and choose the best answer to the questions that follow each one.

(1) Earthquakes occur on the surface of the earth when there is motion in the tectonic plates in the earth's crust. **(2)** The crust of the earth contains twelve such tectonic plates which are from four to ten kilometers in length when located below the sea. **(3)** However, those on land can be from thirty to seventy kilometers long.

(4) Fault lines, the places where these plates meet, build up a great deal of pressure. **(5)** Therefore, the two plates will eventually shift or separate since the pressure on them is constantly increasing, and this build-up of energy needs to be released. **(6)** Therefore, tectonic plates cause earthquakes, both at land and at sea.

(7) When the plates shift or separate, there has been an occurrence of an earthquake, also known as a seismic event. **(8)** The point where the earthquake is at its strongest is called the epicenter. **(9)** In addition, waves of motion travel out from the epicenter, where they cause widespread destruction to an entire geographical area.

(10) With the likelihood for earthquakes to occur, it is essential that earthquake prediction systems are in place. **(11)** The purpose of earthquake prediction is to give advanced warning to the population, thereby saving lives in the process. **(12)** Yet, these prediction systems need to be reliable in order to be of any practical use. **(13)** For this reason, scientists are currently attempting to conduct research on the probability of earthquakes along each of the twelve fault lines.

1. Which is the best version of the underlined portion of sentence 2, reproduced below? **(M)**
    The crust of the earth contains twelve such tectonic <u>plates which</u> are from four to ten kilometers in length when located below the sea.
    A. Leave it as it is now.
    B. plates, which
    C. plates – which
    D. plates, that

Tip: The word "which" forms the beginning of a non-restrictive relative modifying clause. If you are unsure about this concept, please refer back to the grammar guide to learn how to use and punctuate these types of clauses.

2. Sentence 4 is reproduced below.
    Fault lines, the places where these plates meet, build up a great deal of pressure.
    The student is considering adding the following at the end of sentence 4:
    because the plates are constantly pressing on each other
    Should the student make this addition? **(A)**
    A. No, because adding these words would interrupt the flow of the essay.
    B. No, because the paragraph focuses on the build-up of pressure, rather than on the plates.
    C. Yes, because it elaborates on the cause of the increase in pressure, which is discussed in the next sentence.
    D. Yes, because this event fits in with the historical account mentioned in the paragraph.

Tip: For questions on adding text to the paragraph, you need to analyze whether the additional text elaborates on the topic of the paragraph or supports claims made in the text.

3. Which is the most logical placement for sentence 6, reproduced below? **(A)**
   Therefore, tectonic plates cause earthquakes, both at land and at sea.
   A. Where it is now.
   B. After sentence 3.
   C. After sentence 7.
   D. After sentence 9.

Tip: This is a question on maintaining the logical sequence of information and ideas. Sentence 6 mentions earthquakes at land and at sea. To put the sentence in the best place, you need to determine which paragraph describes phenomena both at land and at sea.

4. Which is the best version of the underlined portion of sentence 7, reproduced below?
   When the plates shift or separate, there has been an occurrence of an earthquake, also known as a seismic event. **(M)**
   A. Leave it as it is now.
   B. was
   C. are
   D. is

Tip: This question assesses your knowledge of verb tense. Remember that the present tense is used when describing natural phenomena or scientific facts, as in this paragraph. You may wish to look back at the "Review of Verb Tenses" section of the grammar guide if you need to review these concepts.

5. Which is the best decision regarding the underlined portion of sentence 9, reproduced below?
   In addition, waves of motion travel out from the epicenter, where they cause widespread destruction to an entire geographical area. **(D)**
   A. Leave it as it is now.
   B. Change it to "causing widespread destruction to an entire geographical area."
   C. Place it at the beginning of the sentence.
   D. Delete it and put a period at the end of the new sentence.

Tip: This is a question on identifying problems in modifier placement. When using modifying phrases or clauses, be sure you make clear which word or phrase you are modifying. In this sentence, the waves cause the destruction. Note that the destruction does not occur in the epicenter.

(1) It is often said that every cloud has a silver lining. **(2)** However, when I received word that my application for college had not been accepted, I thought life as I knew it was going to end. **(3)** As I saw the upcoming academic year stretch out in front of me like a deserted highway, I mused, "How could life be so unjust?" **(4)** Little did I know that this delay in my life would ultimately lead to other events.

(5) I will never forget the moment the registrar said, "I'm really sorry, but you've missed the cutoff for this year." **(6)** Had I realized that a simple administrative error on my part was going to delay my studies, I certainly would have been more careful in submitting the necessary forms. **(7)** I was so sure that I was going to be accepted that I had not even bothered to look for work. **(8)** These are the events that led me to embark upon what could have been a year of worry and doubting myself.

(9) However, instead of sinking into a quagmire of thoughts, I decided to take that year as an opportunity to rethink my options. **(10)** I began to ask myself a hard question: "Did I really want to study for the degree program I had chosen?"

(11) I spent weeks scouring the internet for various degree programs and requested a plethora of catalogues from colleges in other states. **(12)** I then narrowed down my options to nine or ten different colleges. **(13)** I also requested financial aid and scholarship information from the colleges I had chosen. **(14)** In the end, three colleges looked the most promising, so I decided to submit applications for admissions, as well as scholarship applications to those places.

(15) The joy I felt when I found out that I had received a full scholarship more than outstripped the agony I had experienced less than a year earlier. **(16)** Had I not had that setback, I never would have decided to pursue a degree in business studies.

6. Which is the best version of the underlined portion of sentence 3, reproduced below? **(M)**
   As I saw the upcoming academic year stretch out in front of me like a deserted highway, I mused, "How could life be so unjust?"
   A. Leave it as it is now.
   B. unjust?
   C. unjust!"
   D. unjust"?

Tip: This is a question on end-of-sentence punctuation. Remember that a question mark should go inside the final quotation mark when the question is part of the original dialogue.

7. Which version of the underlined portion of sentence 4, reproduced below, best introduces the events described in the remainder of the essay? **(A)**
   Little did I know that this delay in my <u>life would ultimately lead to other events.</u>
   A. Leave it as it is now.
   B. life course would ultimately be such a long and winding path.
   C. academic path would ultimately lead to something truly wonderful.
   D. academic pursuits would ultimately lead to several mixed blessings.

Tip: When answering questions on the relevance of word choice to topic and focus, look for the answer that provides the best logical connection of ideas within the essay. In this question, choose the answer that best connects to the writer's academic life, which is described in the main body of the essay, as well as to the writer's receipt of a scholarship, which is described in the conclusion to the essay.

8. Which is the best decision regarding the underlined portion of sentence 8, reproduced below? **(D)**
   These are the events that led me to embark upon what could have been a year of worry and doubting myself.
   A. Leave it as it is now.
   B. of worry and self-doubt.
   C. of: worry and doubting myself.
   D. of worrying and self-doubt.

Tip: This is a question on parallel structure. "Parallel structure" means that you need to use the same parts of speech when you list items in a series. So, all of the items need to be nouns or verbs, for example. In this essay, we are listing two concepts, but "worry" is a noun and "doubting" is a verb.

9. In sentence 9, the writer wants to link to her comments from sentence 8. Which version of the underlined portion of sentence 9, reproduced below, best achieves that goal? **(A)**
   However, instead of sinking into a quagmire of thoughts, I decided to take that year as an opportunity to rethink my options.
   A. worrying
   B. depression
   C. worrying and depression
   D. self-recrimination and anxiety

Tip: When writing topic sentences for each paragraph, you need to maintain the proposition. In other words, there should be a clear flow of ideas or claims from one paragraph to the next. To find the correct answer, determine which answer choice contains synonyms for "self-doubt" and "worry" from the previous sentence.

10. Which choice best combines sentences 12 and 13, reproduced below, at the underlined portion? **(D)**
    I then narrowed down my options to nine or ten different colleges. I also requested financial aid and scholarship information from the colleges I had chosen.
    A. colleges. and I also requested financial aid and scholarship information from the colleges I had chosen.
    B. colleges, and requested financial aid and scholarship information from the colleges I had chosen.
    C. colleges and requested financial aid and scholarship information from them.
    D. colleges, and requested financial aid and scholarship information from them.

Tip: Be sure you know how to coordinate and subordinate sentences and punctuate them correctly for the exam. "Coordination" generally means that you are combining two or more similar ideas within a single sentence. The word "and" is often used to coordinate sentences. You also need to be sure that you know how to punctuate the sentence correctly. Remember that a comma is needed after the word before the word "and" when there is a grammatical subject after the word "and." You also need to be confident about how to subordinate sentences correctly for the exam. "Subordination" means that you are combining different ideas within a single sentence. In contrast to coordination, the ideas are not given equal weight or emphasis in a subordinated sentence; rather, one idea is generally given more emphasis. If you are unsure about these concepts, please refer back to the "Subordination" section of the grammar guide.

(1) In the fall of 1859, a discouraged man was sitting in his run-down law office in Springfield, Illinois. **(2)** He was fifty years old, and he had been a lawyer for twenty years, earning around three thousand dollars a year. **(3)** His tangible possessions and property consisted of 160 acres of farm land in Iowa and the house which he lived in Illinois. **(4)** Although his monetary resources were limited and he was in debt, this man would later go on to do great things for his country. **(5)** His name was Abraham Lincoln.

(6) In 1859, some of Lincoln's associates had already begun to put forward the idea that he should run for president of the United States. **(7)** He discounted the notion in his usual self-deprecating manner. **(8)** Yet, as time passed, Lincoln started to believe that his candidacy for United States President might be possible. **(9)** In order to gain the support of his political party, he began to write to influential Republican Party leaders, including Norman Judd and Richard Oglesby. **(10)** By the end of 1860, Lincoln garnered more public support, after he delivered public lectures and political speeches in various states.

(11) The Republican National Convention took place in Chicago on May 16, 1860. **(12)** William Seward, an outstandingly popular Republican leader, was predicted to win the nomination for the Republican Party. **(13)** Seward's later purchase of Alaska was termed "Seward's folly" and made him the object of political ridicule. **(14)** Nevertheless, Lincoln won 354 of the 466 total votes for nomination. **(15)** Thus, in November, 1860, Lincoln was elected as the President of the United States.

11. Which is the best version of sentence 3, reproduced below? **(D)**
    His tangible possessions and property consisted of 160 acres of farm land in Iowa and the <u>house which he lived in</u> Illinois.
    A. Leave it as it is now.
    B. house; which he lived in
    C. house that he lived in
    D. house in which he lived in

Tip: This is a question on relative clauses. Relative clauses often use the words "who," "that," "which," or "where." Remember that the "in which" construction can be used as a more formal alternative to "where."

12. Which option below best combines sentences 6 and 7, reproduced below, at the underlined portion? **(D)**
    In 1859, some of Lincoln's associates had already begun to put forward the idea that he should run for president of the <u>United States. He discounted the notion</u> in his usual self-deprecating manner.
    A. United States, a notion that he discounted
    B. Unites States, he discounted the notion
    C. United States – this being a notion that he discounted
    D. Unites States, discounting the notion

Tip: In order to combine sentences effectively, you need to look for the repetition of ideas in two subsequent sentences. Here, the words "the notion" refer back to "the idea" in the first part of the previous sentence.

13. Which is the best version of the underlined portion of sentence 9, reproduced below? **(M)**
    <u>In order to gain</u> the support of his political party, he began to write to influential Republican Party leaders, including Norman Judd and Richard Oglesby.
    A. Leave it as it is now.
    B. Thereby, to gain
    C. Whereas, to gain
    D. For example, to gain

Tip: For questions on using transition words and phrases, you need to analyze the relationship between the ideas within a sentence. To carry out this type of analysis, ask yourself the following types of questions: Is the transition word or phrase introducing an example or a reason? Is the answer choice grammatically correct?

14. Which is the best version of the underlined portion of sentence 10, reproduced below? **(D)**
    By the end of 1860, Lincoln garnered more public support, after he <u>delivered</u> public lectures and political speeches in various states.
    A. Leave it as it is now.
    B. had delivered
    C. was delivered
    D. had been delivered

Tip: Verb voice refers to whether a sentence should be written in the active or passive voice. Active voice (e.g. – delivered, had delivered) should be used when you want to emphasize the person who is doing the action. Passive voice (was delivered, had been delivered) should be used when want to emphasize the object or outcome. If you are unsure about these concepts, please refer to the section on verb tense and voice in the grammar guide.

15. Which sentence blurs the focus of the last paragraph and should therefore be deleted from the essay? **(D)**
    A. Sentence 11
    B. Sentence 12
    C. Sentence 13
    D. Sentence 14

Tip: You will be asked to delete sentences that blur the focus of the essay on your writing test. You need to determine the primary focus of the essay to answer these types of questions. Note that in this essay, the focus is on Lincoln, not Seward.

(1) The study of the philosophy of human nature is often regarded as an investigation into the meaning of life. **(2)** This subject deals with four key problem areas: human choice, human thought, human personality and the unity of the human being. **(3)** A consideration of these four problem areas can also include scientific and artistic viewpoints on the nature of human life.

(4) The first problem area, human choice, asks whether a human being can really make decisions that can change their future. **(5)** Conversely, it investigates to what extent the individual's future is fixed and pre-determined by cosmic forces outside the control of the human being.

(6) In the second problem area, human thought, epistemology is considered. **(7)** Epistemology means the study of knowledge, it should not be confused with ontology, the study of being or existence.

(8) The third key issue, human personality, emphasizes aspects of human life that are beyond mental processes. **(9)** It takes a look at emotional, spiritual, and communal elements. **(10)** Importantly, the communal aspect focuses on community and communication, rather than on government or the philosophy of the state.

(11) Finally, the fourth problem area, the unity of the human being, explores the first three areas more fully and asks whether there is any unifying basis for human choice, thought, and personality. **(12)** In other words, humans are inherently complex and multifaceted beings.

16. Which is the best version of the underlined portion of sentence 2, reproduced below? **(M)**
    This subject deals with four key problem <u>areas: human choice, human thought, human personality and the unity of the human being.</u>
    A.   Leave it as it is now.
    B.   areas, human choice, human thought, human personality, and the unity of the human being.
    C.   areas: human choice, human thought, human personality, and the unity of the human being.
    D.   areas; human choice, human thought, human personality and the unity of the human being.

Tip: This is a question on punctuating items in a series. Remember that the colon can be used when several items are listed in a series after it. Also remember that a comma should be used after each word in the series that is before the word "and."

17. Which is the best version of the underlined portion of sentence 4, reproduced below? **(M)**
    The first problem area, human choice, asks whether a human being can really make decisions that can change <u>their future</u>.
    A.   Leave it as it is now.
    B.   their futures
    C.   his or her future
    D.   his or her futures

Tip: This is a question on pronoun person and number. The word being modified is "future," which is singular. So, the possessive pronoun before the word "future" should also be singular. The pronoun refers to "a human being," so the possessive pronoun should be in the third person.

18. Which is the decision regarding the underlined portion of sentence 7, reproduced below? **(M)**
    Epistemology means the study of <u>knowledge, it</u> should not be confused with ontology, the study of being or existence.
    A.   Leave it as it is now.
    B.   Use a colon, instead of a comma.
    C.   Use a semicolon, instead of a comma.
    D.   Insert the word "which" after the comma.

Tip: In order to avoid run-on sentences, you need to identify sentence boundaries. Here we have two complete sentences, the first beginning with "epistemology" and the second beginning with "it." Remember that a semicolon can be used between two complete sentences.

19. Which is the best version of the underlined portion of sentence 8, reproduced below? **(M)**
    The third key issue, human personality, <u>emphasizes</u> aspects of human life that are beyond mental processes.
    A.   Leave it as it is now.
    B.   emphasize
    C.   does emphasize
    D.   will emphasize

Tip: You will need to have agreement between the subject and verb within each sentence in an essay. Note that the grammatical subject of this sentence is "human personality," which is singular. Also be sure to use the correct verb tense.

20. Sentence 12 is reproduced below.
In other words, humans are inherently complex and multifaceted beings.
The student is considering adding the following text at the end of the sentence:
, but there must be a unity or wholeness which underlies these complications
Should the student make this addition there? **(D)**
   A. Yes, because it addresses a rebuttal that was mentioned previously.
   B. Yes, because it links to the idea of a "unifying basis" mentioned in the previous sentence.
   C. No, because it introduces superfluous information into the essay.
   D. No, because it fails to explain the notions of unity and wholeness.

Tip: This question is asking you to choose the best conclusion to the essay. The topic sentence of this final paragraph focuses on the unity of the human being, so look for synonyms for this idea in the new text.

(1) Cancer, a group of more than 100 different types of disease, occurs when cells in the body begin to divide abnormally and continue dividing and forming more cells without control or order. **(2)** All internal organs of the body consist of cells, which normally divide to produce more cells when the body requires them. **(3)** This is a natural, orderly process that keeps human beings healthy.

(4) If cell division occurs when they are not necessary, a large growth called a tumor can form. **(5)** These tumors can usually be removed, and in many cases, they do not recur. **(6)** Unfortunately, in some cases the cancer from the original tumor spreads and effects other parts of the body. **(7)** The spread of cancer in this way is called metastasis.

(8) Research has shown that some factors greatly increase the risk of cancer. **(9)** Smoking is the largest single cause of death, from cancer in the United States. **(10)** One-third of the deaths from cancer each year are related to smoking. **(11)** Making tobacco use the most preventable cause of death in this country.

(12) Choice of food can also be linked to cancer. **(13)** Research shows that there is a link between high-fat food and certain cancers, and being seriously overweight is also a cancer risk. **(14)** Cancer risk can be reduced by cutting down on fatty food and eating generous amounts of fruit and vegetables, which would decrease the chance of getting cancer.

21. Which is the best version of the underlined portion of sentence 4, reproduced below? **(M)**
If cell division occurs when <u>they are</u> not necessary, a large growth called a tumor can form.
   A. Leave it as it is now.
   B. their
   C. are
   D. it is

Tip: For questions on pronoun-antecedent agreement, you need to be sure that the pronoun agrees in number with the grammatical subject of the sentence or clause. Here, the grammatical subject of the sentence is "cell division," which is singular.

22. Which is the best decision regarding the underlined portion of sentence 6, reproduced below? **(D)**
    Unfortunately, in some cases the cancer from the original tumor spreads <u>and effects</u> other parts of the body.
    A. Leave it as it is now.
    B. Change "effects" to "affects"
    C. Change "effects" to "excepts"
    D. Change "effects" to "expects"

Tip: Be sure you know the differences between frequently confused words for the exam. Remember that "affect" is used as a verb meaning resulting in, while "effect" is a noun meaning outcome. If you are unsure about these concepts, please refer to the "commonly confused words" section in the grammar guide.

23. Which is the best version of the underlined portion of sentence 9, reproduced below? **(M)**
    Smoking is the largest single cause of <u>death, from cancer</u> in the United States.
    A. Leave it as it is now.
    B. death—from cancer
    C. cancer death
    D. death from cancer

Tip: This is a question on avoiding unnecessary punctuation. Remember that different rules apply to the punctuation of clauses and phrases within sentences. Please refer to the punctuation and subordination sections of the grammar guide if you are unsure about these concepts.

24. Which choice most effectively combines the underlined portions of sentences 10 and 11, reproduced below? **(M)**
    One-third of the deaths from cancer each year are related to <u>smoking. Making tobacco use</u> the most preventable cause of death in this country.
    A. smoking, which means that tobacco use
    B. smoking tobacco
    C. smoking, making tobacco use
    D. smoking, and tobacco use

Tip: This is a question on sentence fragments. A sentence fragment is not a complete, grammatical sentence because it does not contain both a grammatical subject and verb. A sentence fragment should be joined to the previous or subsequent sentence. Also choose the answer that has the best style.

25. Which is the decision regarding the underlined portion of sentence 14, reproduced below? **(D)**
    Cancer risk can be reduced by cutting down on fatty food and eating generous amounts of fruit and <u>vegetables, which would decrease the chance of getting cancer</u>.
    A. Leave it as it is now.
    B. Change "would decrease" to "decrease" to make the sentence more emphatic.
    C. Place a period after "vegetables" and delete the comma and other underlined text from the sentence.
    D. Change "would decrease" to "decreasing" to make the sentence more concise.

Tip: This question is asking you to improve the concision of the essay. To answer this type of question, you need to determine whether any ideas have been unnecessarily repeated within the sentence or essay.

PUNCTUATION AND CAPITALIZATION REVIEW EXERCISES

Instructions: The draft essay below contains several errors in capitalization and punctuation. Choose the correct version of each part of the sentences from the options provided. If the sentence is correct as written, you should choose answer choice A. **(M)**

[1] It was in 1929, that electrical activity in the human brain was first discovered. [2] Hans Berger, the german psychiatrist who made the discovery, [3] was despondent to find out however that his research was quickly dismissed by many other scientists.

[4] The work of Berger was confirmed three years later, in 1932, when Edgar Adrian a briton, [5] clearly demonstrated that the brain, like the heart, is profuse in its electrical activity. [6] Because of Adrian's work, it is known that the electrical impulses [7] in the brain called brain waves are a mixture of four different frequencies, [8] which are based on the number of identifiable recurring electrical [9] impulses, that occur in the brain per second.

[10] Accordingly, there are four types of brain waves as follows, alpha, beta, delta, and theta. [11] Alpha waves occur in a state of relaxation, while beta waves occur when a person is alert. [12] In addition, delta waves take place during sleep but they can also occur dysfunctionally when the brain has been severely damaged. [13] Finally theta waves are of a frequency [14] somewhere in between alpha and delta. [15] It seems, that the purpose of theta waves is solely to facilitate the combination of the other brain waves.

[16] The whole notion of brain waves feeds into the current controversy about brain death. [17] Some people's belief is that brain death is characterized by the failure of the cerebral cortex to function. [18] On the other hand others say that mere damage to the cerebral cortex is not enough. [19] They assert that brain stem function must also cease before a person can be declared dead because the cerebral cortex is responsible for other bodily processes.

Item 1.
- A. It was in 1929, that electrical activity in the human brain was first discovered.
- B. It was in 1929 that electrical activity in the human brain was first discovered.
- C. It was in 1929, that electrical activity in the human brain, was first discovered.
- D. It was in 1929 that electrical activity, in the human brain was first discovered.
- E. It was in 1929 that electrical activity in the human brain, was first discovered.

Item 2.
- A. Hans Berger, the german psychiatrist who made the discovery,
- B. Hans Berger, the german psychiatrist, who made the discovery,
- C. Hans Berger, the German psychiatrist who made the discovery,
- D. Hans Berger the German psychiatrist who made the discovery,
- E. Hans Berger the German psychiatrist, who made the discovery,

Item 3.
- A. was despondent to find out however that his research was quickly dismissed by many other scientists.
- B. was despondent to find out however, that his research was quickly dismissed by many other scientists.

- C. was despondent to find out, however that his research was quickly dismissed by many other scientists.
- D. was despondent to find out, however, that his research was quickly dismissed by many other scientists.
- E. was despondent to find out; however, that his research was quickly dismissed by many other scientists.

Item 4.
- A. The work of Berger was confirmed three years later, in 1932, when Edgar Adrian a briton,
- B. The work of Berger was confirmed three years later, in 1932, when Edgar Adrian, a Briton,
- C. The work of Berger was confirmed three years later in 1932, when Edgar Adrian a Briton
- D. The work of Berger was confirmed three years later, in 1932, when Edgar Adrian a Briton;
- E. The work of Berger was confirmed three years later in 1932, when Edgar Adrian, a briton;

Item 5.
- A. clearly demonstrated that the brain, like the heart, is profuse in its electrical activity.
- B. clearly demonstrated that the brain like the heart, is profuse in its electrical activity.
- C. clearly demonstrated that the brain like the heart is profuse in its electrical activity.
- D. clearly demonstrated that the brain, like the heart is profuse in its electrical activity.
- E. clearly demonstrated that the brain; like the heart is profuse in its electrical activity.

Item 6.
- A. Because of Adrian's work, it is known that the electrical impulses
- B. Because of Adrian's work it is known that the electrical impulses
- C. Because of Adrian's work: it is known that the electrical impulses
- D. Because of Adrian's work; it is known that the electrical impulses
- E. Because of Adrian's work, it is known, that the electrical impulses

Item 7.
- A. in the brain called brain waves are a mixture of four different frequencies,
- B. in the brain, called brain waves are a mixture of four different frequencies,
- C. in the brain called brain waves, are a mixture of four different frequencies,
- D. in the brain, called brain waves, are a mixture of four different frequencies,
- E. in the brain, called brain waves, are a mixture, of four different frequencies,

Item 8.
- A. which are based on the number of identifiable recurring electrical
- B. which are based on the number of identifiable, recurring, electrical
- C. which are based on the number of identifiable, recurring electrical
- D. which are based on the number of identifiable recurring, electrical
- E. which are based on the number of identifiable, recurring, electrical,

Item 9.
- A. impulses, that occur in the brain per second.
- B. impulses that, occur in the brain per second.
- C. impulses that occur, in the brain per second.
- D. impulses that occur in the brain per second;
- E. impulses that occur in the brain per second.

Item 10.
- A. Accordingly, there are four types of brain waves as follows, alpha, beta, delta, and theta.
- B. Accordingly, there are four types of brain waves as follows: alpha, beta, delta, and theta.
- C. Accordingly, there are four types of brain waves as follows; alpha, beta, delta, and theta.
- D. Accordingly, there are four types of brain waves as follows; Alpha, Beta, Delta, and Theta.
- E. Accordingly, there are four types of brain waves as follows. Alpha, beta, delta, and theta.

Item 11.
- A. Alpha waves occur in a state of relaxation, while beta waves occur when a person is alert.
- B. Alpha waves occur in a state of relaxation while beta waves occur when a person is alert.
- C. Alpha waves occur in a state of relaxation while beta waves occur, when a person is alert.
- D. Alpha waves occur in a state of relaxation, while beta waves occur, when a person is alert.
- E. Alpha waves occur in a state of relaxation; while beta waves occur when a person is alert.

Item 12.
- A. In addition, delta waves take place during sleep but they can also occur dysfunctionally when the brain has been severely damaged.
- B. In addition, delta waves take place during sleep, but they can also occur dysfunctionally when the brain has been severely damaged.
- C. In addition delta waves take place during sleep, but they can also occur dysfunctionally when the brain has been severely damaged.
- D. In addition, Delta Waves take place during sleep, but they can also occur dysfunctionally when the brain has been severely damaged.
- E. In addition, Delta Waves take place during sleep, but they can also occur dysfunctionally, when the brain has been severely damaged.

Item 13.
- A. Finally theta waves are of a frequency
- B. Finally, theta waves are of a frequency
- C. Finally, theta waves are of a frequency,
- D. Finally theta waves are of a frequency,
- E. Finally, theta waves are of a frequency;

Item 14.
- A. somewhere in between alpha and delta.
- B. somewhere, in between, alpha and delta.
- C. somewhere, in between, Alpha and delta.
- D. somewhere in between Alpha and delta.
- E. somewhere in between: alpha and delta.

Item 15.
- A. It seems, that the purpose of theta waves is solely to facilitate the combination of the other brain waves.
- B. It seems that, the purpose of theta waves is solely to facilitate the combination of the other brain waves.
- C. It seems that the purpose of theta waves is solely to facilitate the combination of the other Brain Waves.
- D. It seems, that the purpose of theta waves is solely to facilitate the combination of the other Brain Waves.
- E. It seems that the purpose of theta waves is solely to facilitate the combination of the other brain waves.

Item 16.
- A. The whole notion of brain waves feeds into the current controversy about brain death.
- B. The whole notion of brain waves feeds into the current controversy about Brain Death.
- C. The whole notion of brain waves, feeds into the current controversy about brain death.
- D. The whole notion of brain waves, feeds into the current controversy about Brain Death.
- E. The whole notion of brain waves feeds into, the current controversy about brain death.

Item 17.
- A. Some people's belief is that brain death is characterized by the failure of the cerebral cortex to function.
- B. Some peoples' belief is that brain death is characterized by the failure of the cerebral cortex to function.
- C. Some peoples belief is that brain death is characterized by the failure of the cerebral cortex to function.
- D. Some people's belief is that brain death is characterized by the failure of the Cerebral Cortex to function.
- E. Some peoples' belief is that brain death is characterized by the failure of the Cerebral Cortex to function.

Item 18.
- A. On the other hand others say that mere damage to the cerebral cortex is not enough.
- B. On the other hand, others' say that mere damage to the cerebral cortex is not enough.
- C. On the other hand, others say that mere damage to the cerebral cortex is not enough.
- D. On the other hand, others' say that mere damage to the cerebral cortex is not enough.
- E. On the other hand, other's say that mere damage to the cerebral cortex is not enough.

Item 19.
- A. They assert that brain stem function must also cease before a person can be declared dead because the cerebral cortex is responsible for other bodily processes.
- B. They assert that brain stem function must also cease, before a person can be declared dead because the cerebral cortex is responsible for other bodily processes.
- C. They assert that brain stem function must also cease before, a person can be declared dead because the cerebral cortex is responsible for other bodily processes.
- D. They assert, that brain stem function must also cease before a person can be declared dead because the cerebral cortex is responsible for other bodily processes.
- E. They assert that brain stem function must also cease; before a person can be declared dead because the cerebral cortex is responsible for other bodily processes.

Item 20.
Imagine that the student would like to add the following sentence to the essay. What is the best location for this sentence?
Therefore, for these myriad reasons, it has become very important to measure brain activity.
- A. At the end of the first paragraph.
- B. At the end of the second paragraph.
- C. At the end of the third paragraph.
- D. At the beginning of the last paragraph.
- E. At the end of the last paragraph.

SENTENCE CORRECTION AND REVISION PRACTICE SET 1

Select the best substitute for the underlined parts of the following ten sentences. The first answer [choice A] is identical to the original sentence. If you think the original sentence is best, then choose A as your answer. **(D)**

1. Although only sixteen years old, <u>the university accepted her application because of her outstanding grades</u>.
    A. the university accepted her application because of her outstanding grades.
    B. her application was accepted by the university because of her outstanding grades.
    C. her outstanding grades resulted in her application being accepted by the university.
    D. she was accepted to study at the university because of her outstanding grades.

2. Never in my life <u>have I seen such a beautiful sight.</u>
    A. have I seen such a beautiful sight.
    B. I have seen such a beautiful sight
    C. such a beautiful sight I have seen.
    D. such a beautiful sight I saw.

3. After the loss of a loved one, the bereaved can experience <u>shock, numbness, and they also get depressed.</u>
    A. shock, numbness, and they also get depressed.
    B. shock, numbness, and depression.
    C. shock, numbness, and get depressed.
    D. shock, numbness, and depressed.

4. I was going to study this <u>evening, however the noise next door</u> made it impossible.
    A. evening, however the noise next door
    B. evening: however the noise next door
    C. evening, however, the noise next door
    D. evening. However, the noise next door

5. She was hoping to buy <u>a new car which would be spacious enough to transport</u> her equipment.
    A. a new car which would be spacious enough to transport
    B. a new car, which would be spacious enough to transport
    C. a new car – which would be spacious enough to transport
    D. a new car, that would be spacious enough to transport

6. Near a small <u>river, at the bottom of the canyon we discovered a cave.</u>
    A. river, at the bottom of the canyon we discovered a cave.
    B. river at the bottom of the canyon we discovered a cave.
    C. river at the bottom of the canyon, we discovered a cave.
    D. river, at the bottom of the canyon, we discovered, a cave.

7. <u>Who did the interview panel select</u> for the job?
    A. Who did the interview panel select
    B. Whom did the interview panel select
    C. Who the interview panel selected
    D. Whom the interview panel selected

8. They played <u>the song "Always and Forever"</u> at their wedding reception.
    A. the song "Always and Forever"
    B. the song, "Always and Forever,"

            C.   the song "Always and Forever,"
            D.   the song "Always and Forever",

9.   He lost his scholarship, as a consequence of his poor grades.
            A.   scholarship, as a consequence of his poor grades.
            B.   scholarship as a consequence of his poor grades.
            C.   scholarship, as a consequence his poor grades.
            D.   scholarship, as a consequence of, his poor grades.

10.   If I was a millionaire, I would give money to charity.
            A.   If I was a millionaire, I would give
            B.   If I was a millionaire, I will give
            C.   If I were a millionaire, I would give
            D.   If I were a millionaire, I will give

SENTENCE CORRECTION AND REVISION PRACTICE SET 2

Instructions: Select the best substitute for the underlined parts of the following ten sentences. The first answer [choice A] is identical to the original sentence. If you think the original sentence is best, then choose A as your answer. **(D)**

1.   The child tried to grab the cookies from the shelf, however they were out of reach.
            A.   shelf, however they were
            B.   shelf: however they were
            C.   shelf. However, they were
            D.   shelf however, they were

2.   Covered in chocolate frosting, the hostess dropped the cake in front of all her guests.
            A.   frosting, the hostess dropped the cake
            B.   frosting, the hostess cake dropped
            C.   frosting, the cake was dropped by the hostess
            D.   frosting, by the hostess the cake was dropped

3.   To love and be loved is the greatest happiness of existence.
            A.   To love and be loved
            B.   Loving and be loved
            C.   Loving and to be loved
            D.   To love and being loved

4.   He wanted to buy a telescope, one which he could use to gaze at the stars.
            A.   telescope, one which he could
            B.   telescope, which one he could
            C.   telescope one which he could
            D.   telescope. One which he could

5.   No sooner I had finished gardening than it began to rain.
            A.   I had finished the gardening than
            B.   I finished the gardening than
            C.   had I finished the gardening than
            D.   had finished I the gardening than

6.   If I went out alone after dark, I try to be more alert and careful.
            A.   I went out
            B.   I go out

  C. I had gone out
  D. I were going out

7. "I am not really interested in <u>this movie" he</u> said.
  A. this movie" he
  B. this movie," he
  C. this movie" . he
  D. this movie." He

8. <u>When a person is confused about his or her identity, this</u> is known as an identity crisis.
  A. When a person is confused about his or her identity, this
  B. When you are confused about your identity, this
  C. The experience of confusion about one's own identity, this
  D. The experience of confusion about one's own identity

9. <u>Upset, from receiving the bad news, Mary</u> broke down and cried.
  A. Upset, from receiving the bad news, Mary
  B. Upset, from receiving the bad news Mary
  C. Upset from receiving the bad news, Mary
  D. Upset from receiving the bad news Mary,

10. <u>Dilapidated and disheveled the house appeared</u> forlorn and abandoned.
  A. Dilapidated and disheveled the house appeared
  B. Dilapidated and disheveled the house, appeared
  C. Dilapidated and disheveled the house appeared,
  D. Dilapidated and disheveled, the house appeared

SENTENCE CORRECTION AND REVISION PRACTICE SET 3

Each of the sentences below has four underlined parts. Read each sentence and determine whether any of the underlined parts contains an error in grammar or use. If so, select the underlined part that contains the error as your answer. If the sentence contains no error, then select "No error." No sentence contains more than one error. **(A)**

1. One of the first skyscrapers <u>to be</u> erected in New York, at the site <u>where</u> its television mast would be most effective, the Empire State Building <u>was constructed</u> in the Art Deco style <u>around</u> 1930. <u>No error</u>

2. <u>Even though</u> chicory is usually cooked, <u>their</u> leaves <u>can be eaten</u> in various ways, including as a raw ingredient in salads or <u>as a dried</u> and ground substitute for coffee. <u>No error</u>

3. Many <u>composers</u> promote nationalism in <u>their</u> work, <u>but what</u> is different about Mussorgsky's <u>compositions are</u> the overt patriotism in his operas. <u>No error</u>

4. Lymph glands, masses of tissue <u>that</u> form part of the lymphatic system, filter bacteria and organisms from <u>organ's</u> in the body and allow lymph <u>to flow</u> into capillaries and <u>from</u> them into lymph vessels. <u>No error</u>

5. Scientifically speaking <u>,</u> <u>almost any</u> positive electric charge can <u>produce</u> a unit of energy <u>from which</u> a volt of electricity is derived. <u>No error</u>

6. It is difficult <u>to know</u> <u>when</u> people first began to grow sweet potatoes <u>because</u> early settlers often did not differentiate this vegetable <u>to</u> other tubers. <u>No error</u>

7. Although companies try to price their products competitively, they often cannot , in spite of their best plans, introduce no new merchandise into the market at a profit. No error

8. Commencing in 1847 and for nearly 16 years thereafter, Mexico City was occupied by U.S. troops until it was conquered by Maximilian, a ruler whose name originates from the roman word *maximus*. No error

9. Ratified at the end of 1992 , the North American Free Trade Agreement eliminated trade barriers among Canada and the United States in order to increase trade and to enable each of the counties to find its unique market position. No error

10. Scientists have discovered that most comets in orbit around the sun , seem to be composed of rock and dust particles embedded in ice. No error

11. Since Christopher Columbus believed that he had established a route between the East Indies and China, subsequent explorer's journeys were impeded by all other theories requiring them to think otherwise. No error

12. Some residents of the former East Germany opposed the dismantling of the Berlin Wall, while others despaired of its very existence because many residents die when attempting to cross it. No error

13. Originally focusing on suffrage, the Women's Rights Movement expanded to include much more than the right to vote and effected the role of women in many countries around the world. No error

14. The Inca migration from the Peruvian highlands to the area west of the Andes constitute an example of the consolidation and extension of the tribe's empire in South America. No error

15. When a government establishes a public sector borrowing requirement, it raises money through the issuance of stocks and bonds, which not only increases its available funds and also forms part of the national debt. No error

16. Ceded by the British to the United States in 1783, the Territory of Wisconsin was inhabited by settlers who differed from that of other territories, not settling the region in haste as newcomers to other states did. No error

17. Born in Hamlet , North Carolina, John Coltrane was arguably one of the most famous of all jazz musicians having played the saxophone. No error

18. A rope and pulley system, an everyday apparatus that easily lifts heavy items, having long been recognized by physicists as a useful application of applied force. No error

19. Great Danes, large hunting dogs that were bred originally by Germans, were once the principle companion animal for the wealthy. No error

*Select the best substitute for the **highlighted** parts of the following ten sentences. The first answer [choice A] is identical to the original sentence. If you think the original sentence is best, then choose A as your answer.* **(D)**

20. The name "catfish" is applied to a very large family of freshwater fish called the Siluriformes, which have whisker-like barbels **growing from its mouth**.
    A. growing from its mouth.
    B. growing from it's mouth.

C. growing from their mouths.
D. grown from the mouth.
E. to grow from the mouth.

21. While driving the car this afternoon, **the tire suddenly went flat and I was surprised.**
    A. the tire suddenly went flat and I was surprised.
    B. the tire suddenly went flat, and I was surprised.
    C. I was surprised when the tire suddenly went flat.
    D. it was a surprise when the tire suddenly went flat.
    E. it was a surprise as the tire suddenly went flat.

22. Best known for his science fiction classic *Star Wars*, US film producer and director George Lucas was revolutionary at the time for having worked with Francis Ford Coppola, retaining the merchandising rights for his works, **and the special effects to be used in his movies.**
    A. and the special effects to be used in his movies.
    B. and using special effects in his movies.
    C. and the special effects used in his movies.
    D. and the special effects he used in his movies.
    E. and used special effects in his movies.

23. We were planning a picnic for the kids in the park **this afternoon, the rain made it impossible.**
    A. this afternoon, the rain made it impossible.
    B. this afternoon, the rain making it impossible.
    C. this afternoon, with the rain made it impossible.
    D. this afternoon, but the rain made it impossible.
    E. this afternoon, it was the rain that made it impossible.

24. It is said that Roosevelt's favorite pursuits were **to read, play games, and doing crossword puzzles.**
    A. to read, play games, and doing crossword puzzles.
    B. to read, games, and crossword puzzles.
    C. reading, gaming and do crossword puzzles.
    D. reading, games, and doing crossword puzzles
    E. reading, playing games, and doing crossword puzzles.

25. **Being frustrated and fed up, and tired from a hard week at work,** she decided it was time to go away on vacation.
    A. Being frustrated and fed up, and tired from a hard week at work,
    B. Being frustrated and fed up, and she was tired from a hard week at work,
    C. With being frustrated and fed up, and tired from a hard week at work,
    D. Frustrated, fed up, and tired from a hard week at work,
    E. Frustrated and fed up, and also tired from a hard week at work,

26. With his unconventional style, E.E. Cummings inspired a generation of experimental artists called "avant-garde poets," **who disregarded poetic form and rebelling** against the use of traditional spelling and punctuation in verse.
    A. who disregarded poetic form and rebelling
    B. who disregarding poetic form and rebelling
    C. who disregarded poetic form and rebelled
    D. to disregard poetic form and rebelling
    E. who, disregarding poetic form to rebel

27. An outstanding military commander and statesman, George Washington **having strictly avoided** overstepping the constitutional limitations of presidential power.
    A. having strictly avoided
    B. having to strictly avoid
    C. has strictly avoided
    D. was strictly avoiding
    E. strictly avoided

28. Dolomite, otherwise known as calcium-magnesium carbonate, is one of many minerals in **sedimentary rock forming crystals** and to be used for ornamental purposes.
    A. sedimentary rock forming crystals
    B. sedimentary rock formations of crystals
    C. sedimentary rock to form crystals
    D. sedimentary rock having formed crystals
    E. sedimentary rock that had formed crystals

29. **Despite the fact he worked overtime several days in a row the congressman** didn't finish his report on time.
    A. Despite the fact he worked overtime several days in a row the congressman
    B. Despite the fact that he worked overtime several days in a row, the congressman
    C. In spite of the fact working overtime several days in a row, the congressman
    D. Although overtime was worked several days in a row, the congressman
    E. He worked overtime several days in a row, however the congressman

30. **If text messaging while at the wheel** you could be charged with dangerous driving in some states.
    A. If text messaging while at the wheel
    B. While text messaging at the wheel,
    C. If you text message while at the wheel,
    D. If you text messaging while at the wheel,
    E. Text messaging at the wheel

SENTENCE CORRECTION AND REVISION PRACTICE SET 4

Instructions for Questions 1 to 19 – Each of the sentences below has four underlined parts. Read each sentence and determine whether any of the underlined parts contains an error in grammar or use. If so, select the underlined part that contains the error as your answer. If the sentence contains no error, then select "No error." No sentence contains more than one error. **(A)**

1. Geologists have noted that petroleum is a chemical compound consisting of a complex mixture of hydrocarbons , that appear to be formed from the bodies of long-dead organisms. No error

2. Magnetism occurs when a current is associated with a field of force and with a north-south polarity, which means that any substance tends to align themselves with the field. No error

3. Charlemagne was crowned King of the Franks in 768, and for approximately 46 years afterwards, he engaged in a brutal conquest of Europe, including the campaign against the moorish people in Spain. No error

4. While both the Black Mountain Poets and the Beat Poets shunned social convention through their experimental art forms, the Black Mountain Poets were affiliated with the Black Mountain College in North Carolina, whereas the Beat Poets were concentrated in California. No error

5. <u>Situated at</u> the site <u>where</u> the Pacific Ocean meets the San Francisco Bay, the Golden Gate <u>spanned</u> by its now-famous bridge <u>,</u> which was completed in 1937. <u>No error</u>

6. <u>Although</u> epiphytes are plants which <u>used</u> other plants for support, they are not parasitic because <u>they</u> have broad leaves that catch water as <u>it</u> drips through the canopy of the tropical forest. <u>No error</u>

7. Theoretically _ bacterial meningitis is far more serious <u>than</u> the viral form of the disease, even though viral meningitis, <u>like any</u> viral disease, can result in an infection <u>for which</u> antibiotics will be ineffective. <u>No error</u>

8. He was desperate <u>to improve</u> his grades before graduation <u>;</u> However, he could not, due to the <u>constant</u> distraction from after-school activities, see <u>any</u> academic progress. <u>No error</u>

9. It is possible <u>to predict</u> when lightening <u>will occur</u> because sparks between clouds and the ground <u>are accompanied</u> by light before they are <u>seen as</u> lightening . <u>No error</u>

10. Because <u>it evaluates</u> a <u>horse's</u> ability to execute defined movements, the equestrian disciplines of showjumping and dressage are set in a confined area with everything <u>required</u> <u>for</u> the events in place. <u>No error</u>

11. By the end of 1930 <u>,</u> the International Astrological Union <u>had assigned</u> boundaries on the celestial sphere and <u>grouped</u> stars <u>into</u> 88 constellations. <u>No error</u>

12. John F. Kennedy was <u>indisputably</u> the <u>most important</u> U.S. president <u>having been assassinated</u> during his brief tenure in the <u>Oval Office</u>. <u>No error</u>

13. DDT, an organic compound formerly used in insecticides, was withdrawn from the market <u>because it</u> was highly toxic and <u>proved</u> to have a long-lasting negative impact <u>with</u> the environment. <u>No error</u>

14. When Alexander Graham Bell <u>invented</u> the acoustic telegraph, little did he know that he would <u>not only</u> be known for his <u>experiments</u> with sound, but also <u>going</u> down in history as the father of the modern telephone. <u>No error</u>

15. Harmonic accompaniment, a sound sequence <u>that make</u> a recognizable pattern, has been <u>understood by</u> musicians as <u>nearly always</u> being <u>subordinate to</u> melody. <u>No error</u>

16. <u>Normally</u> grown <u>in</u> warm climates, many types of melons <u>are cultivated</u> in greenhouses nowadays, even out of <u>their</u> usual growing seasons. <u>No error</u>

17. The Hawaiian king Kamehameha _ who was <u>descended from</u> Kamehameha IV, abandoned the Hawaiian constitution and <u>imparted</u> fewer rights to his subjects, <u>as all</u> royal rulers did. <u>No error</u>

18. <u>With</u> books in print in more than 100 countries, Mark Twain's work has had <u>his</u> share of <u>admirers'</u>, as well as an <u>abundance of</u> critics. <u>No error</u>

19. The longest river in the world, the Nile flows <u>from</u> <u>its</u> headstream to the <u>Mediterranean</u> delta in <u>Northeast</u> Egypt. <u>No error</u>

*Instructions for Questions 20 to 30 – Select the best substitute for the **highlighted** parts of the following ten sentences. The first answer [choice A] is identical to the original sentence. If you think the original sentence is best, then choose A as your answer.* **(D)**

20. The defining characteristics of colleges formed during the Antebellum Period **included its** solicitation of government support, promotion of educational opportunities, and provision for educational and technical students.
    A. included its
    B. included their
    C. includes its
    D. includes their
    E. including the

21. Franz Kafka was one of a handful of European novelists **overcoming** intense self-doubt and see his work published during his lifetime.
    A. overcoming
    B. having overcome
    C. who had overcome
    D. to have overcome
    E. to overcome

22. Non-tariff barriers threaten free trade and limit a country's commerce by impeding **its ability to export, to invest, and their financial growth.**
    A. its ability to export, to invest, and their financial growth.
    B. their ability to export, to invest, and financial growth.
    C. it's ability to export, to invest, and their financial growth.
    D. its ability to export, to invest, and financial growth.
    E. its ability to export, to invest, and to grow financially.

23. The first woman elected to the U.S. Congress, suffragist and pacifist Jeannette Rankin **was stanchly promoting** women's rights during her career.
    A. was stanchly promoting
    B. was promoting stanchly
    C. staunchly promoted
    D. having staunchly promoted
    E. having to staunchly promote

24. The diplomat **mailed the letter to the embassy containing confidential information.**
    A. mailed the letter to the embassy containing confidential information.
    B. mailed the letter to the embassy, containing confidential information.
    C. mailed, containing confidential information, the letter to the embassy.
    D. mailed the letter containing confidential information to the embassy.
    E. containing confidential information, mailed the letter to the embassy.

25. Providing an alternative to other energy sources, nuclear power addresses concerns about **increasing air pollution, decreasing fossil fuels, and helps to control costs associated with rising inflation.**
    A. increasing air pollution, decreasing fossil fuels, and helps to control costs associated with rising inflation.
    B. increasing air pollution, decreasing fossil fuels, and help to control costs associated with rising inflation.
    C. increasing air pollution, decreasing fossil fuels, and controlling costs associated with rising inflation.
    D. increasing air pollution, decreasing fossil fuels, and associated costs with rising inflation.

E. increasing air pollution, decreasing fossil fuels, and associating costs with rising inflation.

26. **Drafting the *Declaration of Independence* and serving as Secretary of State,** Thomas Jefferson has a prominent place in US history.
    A. Drafting the *Declaration of Independence* and serving as Secretary of State,
    B. Drafting the *Declaration of Independence*, and he served as Secretary of State,
    C. By drafting the *Declaration of Independence*, and he served as Secretary of State,
    D. Drafting the *Declaration of Independence* and to serve as Secretary of State,
    E. With drafting the *Declaration of Independence*, he served as Secretary of State and,

27. **Honeysuckle is a well-known species of climbing plant native to the northern hemisphere and consequently** often grown for ornamental purposes in patios and gardens.
    A. Honeysuckle is a well-known species of climbing plant native to the northern hemisphere and consequently
    B. Honeysuckle is a well-known species of climbing plant native to the northern hemisphere and thus
    C. Honeysuckle is a well-known species of climbing plant native to the northern hemisphere and furthermore
    D. Since honeysuckle is a well-known species of climbing plant native to the northern hemisphere, it is
    E. Honeysuckle is a well-known species of climbing plant native to the northern hemisphere and because it is

28. **Overworked and underpaid many employees seek** help from their union representatives.
    A. Overworked and underpaid many employees seek
    B. Overworked and underpaid, many employees seek
    C. Overworked and underpaid many employees seek,
    D. Overworked, and underpaid many employees seek
    E. Overworked and underpaid many employees, seek

29. With its sub-zero temperatures and frozen landscape, **hardly no one considers Siberia to be the ideal tourist destination.**
    A. hardly no one considers Siberia to be the ideal tourist destination.
    B. no one hardly considers Siberia to be the ideal tourist destination.
    C. hardly no one considers Siberia as the ideal tourist destination.
    D. no one considers Siberia hardly to be the ideal tourist destination.
    E. Siberia can hardly be considered to be the ideal tourist destination.

30. **When air rises and condenses into precipitation, this phenomenon** is known as a low-pressure system.
    A. When air rises and condenses into precipitation, this
    B. When air rises and condenses into precipitation, this phenomenon
    C. The phenomenon of air rising and condensing into precipitation, this
    D. The phenomenon of air rising and condensing into precipitation
    E. When air rises and condenses into precipitation, a phenomenon which

COMBINING SENTENCES AND IDENTIFYING FRAGMENTS

For questions 1 to 3, choose the sentence that is correctly written. **(D)**

1. A. To love and be loved for great happiness.
    B. A hot summer day in the middle of July.
    C. Swinging wildly from branch to branch.
    D. The restaurant closes at midnight.

2. A. Fat and skinny and all kinds of people.
    B. Should be finishing then?
    C. The cat who goes from house to house.
    D. Off we go on another adventure!

3. A. Another beautiful day in the neighborhood!
    B. A small puddle under the garage door.
    C. He hopes to start this summer.
    D. Leaving at about 6:00 this evening.

For questions 4 to 6, choose the new sentence that correctly and effectively joins the original sentences. **(A)**

4. The temperature was quite high yesterday.
    It really didn't feel that hot outside.
    We decided to go out.
    A. In spite of the temperature being quite high yesterday, it really didn't feel that hot outside, so we decided to go out.
    B. Although we went out yesterday, the temperature was quite high and it really didn't feel hot outside.
    C. Even though it didn't feel hot outside, we went outside in spite of the temperature being quite high yesterday.
    D. We decided to go out in spite of the temperature being quite high yesterday, and it really didn't feel that hot outside.

5. Our star athlete was in the Olympics.
    He had trained for the competition for several years in advance.
    He didn't win a gold medal.
    A. Despite having trained for the competition for several years in advance, our star athlete didn't receive a gold medal in the Olympics.
    B. Our star athlete didn't receive a gold medal, but he had trained for the competition for several years in advance when he went to the Olympics.
    C. He had trained for the competition for several years in advance of the Olympics, although our star athlete didn't receive a gold medal.
    D. In the Olympics, he didn't receive a gold medal, and our star athlete had trained for the competition for several years.

6. There are acrimonious relationships within our extended family.
    Our immediate family decided to go away on vacation during the holiday season.
    We wanted to avoid these conflicts.
    A. To avoid these conflicts because there are acrimonious relationships within our extended family, our immediate family decided to go away on vacation during the holiday season.
    B. Because of acrimonious relationships within our extended family, our immediate family decided to go away on vacation during the holiday season to avoid these conflicts.

C. Due to the fact that there are acrimonious relationships within our extended family, to avoid these conflicts, our immediate family decided to go away on vacation during the holiday season.
D. To avoid these conflicts since our immediate family decided to go away on vacation during the holiday season, there are acrimonious relationships within our extended family.

For questions 7 to 9, choose the sentence that is correctly written. **(D)**

7. A. Just not good for anything is this world.
    B. Staying alert after 11:00 at night is difficult.
    C. Going to see my grandma this weekend.
    D. The college's department of business administration.

8. A. Eat your meal and be quiet!
    B. Always talking nonstop without listening to others.
    C. Huge stresses in life from all sorts of things.
    D. Eating pizza, cookies, and cake all day long.

9. A. Hoping for a miracle and trying to stay positive.
    B. With a better system that will be installed in the spring.
    C. Lovely though it may seem, vacationing overseas can come with problems.
    D. To keep a business afloat during tough financial times.

For questions 10 to 12, choose the new sentence that correctly and effectively joins the original sentences. **(A)**

10. My best friend had been feeling extremely sick for several days.
    She was stubborn.
    She refused to see the doctor.
    A. My best friend had been feeling extremely sick for several days, but she was stubborn and refused to see the doctor.
    B. My best friend, who was stubborn, had been feeling extremely sick for several days, yet she refused to see the doctor.
    C. My best friend had been feeling extremely sick and stubborn for several days, but she refused to see the doctor.
    D. My stubborn best friend refused to see the doctor, and had been feeling extremely sick for several days.

11. He generally doesn't enjoy drinking alcohol.
    He really doesn't like the taste of it.
    He will drink only on social occasions.
    A. While he generally doesn't enjoy drinking alcohol, he will do so on social occasions, and he really doesn't like the taste of it.
    B. He will drink alcohol on social occasions, but he generally doesn't enjoy drinking it and really doesn't like the taste of it.
    C. Although he generally doesn't enjoy drinking alcohol because he doesn't like the taste of it, he will do so on social occasions.
    D. He really doesn't like the taste of alcohol, but he generally doesn't enjoy it, even on social occasions.

12. The government has made some new policies.
    The policies failed to stimulate spending and expand economic growth.
    The country has slipped further into recession.
    A. The government's policies failed, in spite of being new, and did not stimulate spending and expand economic growth, so the country has slipped further into recession.

B. The country has slipped further into recession because the policies failed to stimulate spending and expand economic growth, which were new.
C. The government's policies caused the country to slip further into recession because they were new and failed to stimulate spending and expand economic growth.
D. The government's new policies failed to stimulate spending and expand economic growth, so the country has slipped further into recession.

For questions 13 to 15, choose the sentence that is correctly written. **(D)**

13. A. Before we even realized or understood it.
     B. Away we go to grandmother's house!
     C. Looking intelligent and sophisticated with his glasses on.
     D. The last chance before they move to Denver.

14. A. The old, the new, the borrowed, and the blue are all here.
     B. Studying while working a full-time job.
     C. Shouldn't cost the earth, should it?
     D. A cow grazing peacefully in the field.

15. A. Time and time again without fail!
     B. The summertime concerts at 5:00 in the park.
     C. Talking without listening can lead to misunderstandings.
     D. Gently giving way in the gentle spring wind.

For questions 16 to 18, choose the new sentence that correctly and effectively joins the original sentences. **(A)**

16. Students may need prerequisites for some classes.
     Students may attend other classes without fulfilling a prerequisite.
     However, students are advised that non-required introductory classes are beneficial.
     A. Students are advised of the benefit of non-required introductory courses, although they may attend their classes without fulfilling prerequisites.
     B. Even though students may attend certain classes without fulfilling a prerequisite, they are advised of the benefit of non-required introductory courses.
     C. While students are advised of the benefit of non-required introductory courses, some classes need a prerequisite, but others don't need this.
     D. Even though they may attend some classes by fulfilling a prerequisite, students are advised of the benefit of non-required introductory courses, but this doesn't apply to all classes.

17. There have been advances in technology.
     Medical science has also improved recently.
     Because of this, infant mortality rates have declined substantially in recent years.
     A. Owing to advances in technology and medical science, infant mortality rates have declined substantially in recent years.
     B. Since infant mortality rates have declined substantially in recent years, there have been advances in technology and medical science.
     C. While infant mortality rates have declined substantially in recent years, there have been improvements in technology and medical science has also advanced.
     D. There have been improvements in technology and medical science has also advanced, leading to infant mortality rates declining substantially in recent years.

18. It was the most expensive restaurant in town.
    It provided the worst service.
    The staff was also rude to customers.
    A. It was the most expensive restaurant in town, besides having rude staff and providing the worst service.
    B. In addition to being the most expensive restaurant in town, it had rude staff because it provided the worst service.
    C. The expensive restaurant had rude, terrible servers.
    D. Although having rude staff and providing the worst service, it was the most expensive restaurant in town

For questions 19 to 21, choose the sentence that is correctly written. **(D)**

19. A. They're all here to report for duty.
    B. Pinching pennies and saving every day.
    C. Clearing up the issue once and for all.
    D. Even without considering all of the information.

20. A. Character flaws, warts and all.
    B. Being caring is in her nature.
    C. To honor her for her achievements.
    D. Living in New York while working as an actor.

21. A. Just as mother nature intended.
    B. Reading and swimming are favorite pastimes.
    C. Although you never intended to do so.
    D. Getting by in this world, in spite of its dangers.

For questions 22 to 25, choose the new sentence that correctly and effectively joins the original sentences. **(A)**

22. Tom filled out the application form.
    He sent it to the college.
    He finally got his acceptance letter.
    A. Once he filled out the application form, Tom finally got his acceptance letter after he had sent it in.
    B. Sending his application form to college after filling it out, Tom finally got his acceptance letter.
    C. Receiving his acceptance letter, Tom had filled out the application and sent it in.
    D. After filling out the application form and sending it to college, Tom finally got his acceptance letter.

23. There was excessive rain yesterday.
    Water began to gather in the streets.
    The whole town was flooded.
    A. Because the whole town was flooded, there was excessive rain yesterday and water began to gather in the streets.
    B. There was excessive rain yesterday, so the whole town was flooded and water began to gather in the streets.
    C. Due to excessive rain yesterday, which resulted in water beginning to gather in the streets, the whole town was flooded.
    D. Water began to gather in the streets since the whole town was flooded with excessive rain yesterday.

24. The judge did not punish the criminal justly.
    He decided to grant a lenient sentence.
    This will not deter potential offenders in the future.
    A. Instead of punishing the criminal justly and thereby sending out a message to deter potential offenders in the future, the judge decided to grant a lenient sentence.
    B. Rather than granting a lenient sentence and punishing the criminal justly, the judge sent out a message to deter potential offenders in the future.
    C. Although not granting a lenient sentence and punishing the criminal justly, the judge nevertheless did not send out a message to deter potential offenders in the future.
    D. In order to grant a lenient sentence and punish the criminal justly, the judge sent out a message to deter potential offenders in the future.

25. Which is the best way to combine the two following sentences?

    She worked on her presentation all night in order to be sure that her case was compelling.
    Her audience was discerning and needed to be persuaded about the efficacy of her proposal.

    A. She worked on her presentation all night in order to be sure that her case was compelling, but her audience was discerning and needed to be persuaded about the efficacy of her proposal.
    B. She worked on her presentation all night in order to be sure that her case was compelling; moreover, her audience was discerning and needed to be persuaded about the efficacy of her proposal.
    C. Due to the fact that her audience was discerning and needed to be persuaded about the efficacy of her proposal, she worked on her presentation all night in order to be sure that her case was compelling.
    D. She worked on her presentation all night because her case was compelling and so that her discerning audience could be persuaded.

IDENTIFYING CORRECTLY-WRITTEN WORDS AND SENTENCES

Instructions: Answer the following questions about sentence structure and spelling.

1. Which of the following sentences uses correct parallel structure? **(D)**
   A. The vacation was fun, exciting, and gave me a great chance to unwind.
   B. I went jet skiing, surfing, and also snorkeled for the first time on our vacation.
   C. The hotel was elegant, comfortable, and the staff members were so friendly.
   D. I enjoyed our hotel room, relaxed in the spa, and ate some truly delicious, well-balanced meals on our vacation.

2. Which one of the following sentences has correct subject-verb agreement? **(A)**
   A. The knives or the forks goes into that drawer.
   B. Neither Marisa nor Amy are home.
   C. Each of the men is very strong and determined.
   D. Every one of the books are on the shelf.

3. Read the sentence and answer the question.
   They told me that I would pass my driving test, but I didn't believe it.
   Which of the following sentences is the <u>best</u> revision of the one above? **(A)**
   A. I knew I wouldn't pass my driving test.
   B. I doubted whether I would pass my driving test.
   C. I was skeptical about my driving test.
   D. The result of my driving test was dubious.

4. What is the <u>best</u> replacement for the underlined words in the following sentence? **(D)**
   The teacher asked me to <u>speak up</u> because she could not hear me.
   A. speak more loudly
   B. speak more louder
   C. speak more loud
   D. speak louder

5. Which of the following sentences is written correctly? **(A)**
   A. The group lost their enthusiasm for the project.
   B. The class hopes to elect Shanika as its representative.
   C. A student needs to study hard in order to pass their final exams.
   D. If my friends need anything, he or she can call me anytime.

6. Which of the following sentences uses correct parallel structure? **(D)**
   A. My brother likes to tell stories as well as reading.
   B. My car was damaged on the hood, fender, and on the bumper.
   C. She brought along cookies, as well as cake.
   D. My mother, friend, and the neighbor congratulated me on passing the exam.

7. Read the sentence and answer the question.
   My mother's car (I crashed it last month) was still very annoyed about the money not being reimbursed and called the insurance company to complain.
   Which of the following is the <u>best</u> revision of the sentence? **(A)**
   A. My mother was still very annoyed about the money not being reimbursed for the accident I had with her car, so she called the insurance company to complain.
   B. My mother was still annoyed about the accident that I had with her car, and she called the insurance company to complain that the money hadn't been reimbursed.

    C.   My mother whose car I crashed last month was annoyed about the money not being reimbursed and called the insurance company to complain.
    D.   The accident I had with the car was so annoying to my mother, and she called the insurance company to complain.

8. Which is the best way to combine the two following sentences? **(A)**
Three-dimensional graphic software has been placed on the computers in science lab. The teacher wanted us learn how to render images with the most up-to-date computer program.
    A.   Three-dimensional graphic software has been placed on the computers in science lab, so the teacher wanted us learn how to render images with the most up-to-date computer program.
    B.   The teacher wanted us learn how to render images with the most up-to-date computer program since three-dimensional graphic software has been placed on the computers in science lab.
    C.   Three-dimensional graphic software has been placed on the computers in science lab, so that the most up-to-date computer images can be rendered.
    D.   Three-dimensional graphic software has been placed on the computers in science lab because the teacher wanted us to learn how to render images with the most up-to-date computer program.

9. Read the sentence and answer the question.
The company was obligated to pay tax to the United States, but it moved its bank account to Belize to get around having to do so.
Which one of the following sentences expresses the same idea more concisely? **(A)**
    A.   The company moved its bank account to Belize, so it didn't have to pay tax.
    B.   The company moved its bank account to Belize to evade payment of tax to the United States.
    C.   Because its bank account was in Belize, the company didn't have to pay US tax.
    D.   The company should have paid income tax, but it did not do so, because it moved its bank account to Belize in order to avoid it.

10. Which of the following sentences uses clear pronouns? **(A)**
    A.   Her intelligence and personality make her a great candidate for the job, which is so inspiring.
    B.   Many students in my class like to go to parties, although I do not like them.
    C.   Every person in my class has to give a presentation, so I did mine on the Civil Rights Movement.
    D.   My bus did not arrive at the right time for me to attend the interview, so I missed it.

11. Which of the following sentences is written correctly? **(A)**
    A.   All of the elected officials need to be mindful of the opinions of his or her constituents.
    B.   Either Juan or Brett are going to the movie with me.
    C.   Each of the students has to hand in his or her application by the deadline.
    D.   A group of dissents who disagree with the government's policies have decided to revolt.

12. Which of the following sentences uses correct parallel structure? **(D)**
    A.   I woke up, got out of bed, and drank a coffee.
    B.   I went to the concert with Marti, Akiko, and Sarah was also there.
    C.   I ordered my meal, waited for my drink, and it took so long for it to come.
    D.   The teacher explained the situation to me, clearly, calmly, and without becoming impatient.

13. Read the sentence and answer the question.
    She did not directly say what she meant. She expected me to judge how she felt from her tone of voice.
    Which of the following revisions expresses the same idea more concisely? **(A)**
    A. She was just beating around the bush.
    B. She spoke to me harshly, without coming to the point.
    C. I was supposed to judge her attitude indirectly.
    D. She expected me to infer what she meant.

14. Which of the following sentences is written correctly? **(A)**
    A. If my brothers need help, he can just drop by anytime.
    B. The band members worked together to ensure that they had a good performance.
    C. The town council was pleased when it got the approval for their new offices to be built.
    D. A person should eat well and get enough sleep in order to improve their health.

15. Read the sentence and then answer the question.
    The client's claim the lawyer defended last month was very happy with the outcome of the case and she wrote a positive online review about the law firm.
    Which of the following is the best revision of the sentence above? **(A)**
    A. The client (whose claim the lawyer defended last month) was so happy with the outcome of the case that she wrote a positive online review about the law firm.
    B. The client's claim the lawyer defended last month was very happy with the outcome of the case, and so she wrote a positive online review about the law firm to say so.
    C. The client's claim was very happy with the outcome of the case by the lawyer who defended it who last month and she wrote a positive online review about the law firm.
    D. The client was very happy with the outcome of her case, which the lawyer defended last month, so she wrote a positive online review about the law firm.

For questions 16 to 20, read the text below and make any necessary corrections.

Dear Team:

(1) Thank you for your continuing hard work and dedication. **(2)** There are some exciting changes coming to our department that I wish to alert you to.

(3) Due to Maxim Inc.'s recent acquisition of our company, the executive management had decided that some restructuring of our department is in order so that our transition through this merger can be as seamless as possible.

(4) This is, in general, very good news for all of us since we will be taking ten new sales representatives on board. **(5)** This increase in staff would both relieve our current understaffing situation and prepare us for the heightened sales operations that this merger is anticipated to trigger.

(6) I am scheduling a staff meeting for tomorrow from 12 pm to 1 pm which I will outline the steps of this important transition; lunch will be provided.

Please feel free to reach out to me at any time during the next few weeks with any question or concerns.

Best regards,

Darnell Hobbs
Email: dhobbs@maximinc.com

16. What change, if any, is needed in sentences 1 and 2? **(M)**
    A. Change the second period to a question mark.
    B. Change "dedication" to "dedacation"
    C. Change "coming" to "are coming"
    D. Make no change

17. What change, if any, is needed in sentence 3? **(M)**
    A. Change "had" to "has"
    B. Change "through" to "thru"
    C. Change "seamless" to "seemless"
    D. Make no change

18. What change, if any, is needed in sentence 4? **(M)**
    A. Remove all commas.
    B. Change "since" to "yet"
    C. Change "is" to "was"
    D. Make no change

19. What change, if any, is needed in sentence 5? **(M)**
    A. Change "would" to "will"
    B. Change "understaffing" to "understaffed"
    C. Change "that" to "which"
    D. Make no change

20. What change, if any, is needed in sentence 6? **(M)**
    A. Change "which" to "when"
    B. Change "this" to "that"
    C. Change "anticipated" to "anticapated"
    D. Make no change

WORD MEANING, RELATIONSHIPS, AND CONTEXT

Instructions: For sentences 1 to 12, choose the sentence in which the underlined word has the same meaning as it does in the original sentence. **(A)**

1. My back began to ache after standing up for such a long time.
   A. She had a dull ache in her back for days after the accident.
   B. If you don't have correct posture, you will get an ache in your neck.
   C. Your feet will ache if your shoes are too small.
   D. Having an ache or pain each day is part of the aging process.

2. The police will comb the site of the incident to look for clues.
   A. You need to comb your hair to make a good impression.
   B. We are going to comb through your things until we find your missing keys.
   C. The comb was on top of the dresser with a brush and mirror.
   D. The rooster had an enormous red comb on the top of its head.

3. We are going to fly to London for vacation next year.
   A. An annoying fly kept buzzing around the house.
   B. You can't just expect to study for your exam on the fly.
   C. The mosquitoes will just fly around us unless we light these candles.
   D. He looked really fly wearing his new sunglasses.

4. Tools and hardware are usually made of iron and other metals.
   A. I need to buy an iron and a toaster when I move into my new apartment.
   B. Rail lines usually consist of reinforced iron and wooden railway ties.
   C. We need to iron out our problems before we can move forward.
   D. Having to iron shirts and other items of clothing is such a chore!

5. She is hoping to milk the company for a good settlement for her injury.
   A. Milk and other dairy products have really gone up in price lately.
   B. He is going to milk that situation for all he can.
   C. I am going to learn how to milk a cow when I stay at my aunt's farm.
   D. You need to drink milk to get enough calcium in your diet.

6. The matter under consideration is complex and multi-faceted.
   A. Scientists are working hard to understand the mysteries of dark matter.
   B. The lawyer will look into this legal matter prior to going to court.
   C. What is the matter with you today?
   D. These mistakes are minor and really don't matter.

7. We need to be able to trust one another in this relationship.
   A. All of the money was being held in trust.
   B. I would trust him with my life.
   C. The trust between us has died after she betrayed me so badly.
   D. Access to the trust fund will be granted when he turns 18.

8. All of the students were present for the group assembly.
   A. I got a really nice present from my parents for my birthday.
   B. The chairperson will present you with the award at the ceremony.
   C. You need to count how my members are absent, as well as how many are present.
   D. At the present moment, I don't have an opinion on this issue.

9. The soldier will <u>report</u> for duty when called by the superior officer.
   A. The financial <u>report</u> stated the income and expenses of the company.
   B. There was a <u>report</u> about an accident on the radio this morning.
   C. The shotgun has a very loud <u>report</u> when it is fired.
   D. I need to <u>report</u> for work at 9:00 AM on Saturday.

10. The international <u>trade</u> agreement abolished taxes between the two nations.
    A. The team will <u>trade</u> that baseball player for another.
    B. Did you get a good <u>trade</u> in for your car?
    C. The <u>trade</u> embargo will take effect next month.
    D. His business did a good <u>trade</u> for many years.

11. If you <u>scratch</u> my back, I'll scratch yours.
    A. There was a large <u>scratch</u> on the top of the dresser.
    B. My speaking skills in Spanish really aren't up to <u>scratch</u>.
    C. I always want to <u>scratch</u> mosquito bites, even though I shouldn't.
    D. He had a <u>scratch</u> on his arm after doing all of the gardening.

12. The <u>produce</u> from that ranch is top-notch in quality.
    A. I love eating berries and other fresh <u>produce</u> in the springtime.
    B. I am going to need to work harder in order to <u>produce</u> the desired outcome.
    C. She will help <u>produce</u> the movie by giving her time and money.
    D. The factory will <u>produce</u> 100,000 units by the end of the year.

13. Which of the following sentences uses the underlined word correctly?
    A. Failure to study will <u>effect</u> your grades.
    B. A scientific <u>principal</u> is a concise mathematical statement about the relationship of one object to another.
    C. The run-away thief <u>eluded</u> the police officer.
    D. He thought he saw an oasis in the desert, but it was an optical <u>allusion</u>.

14. Which one of the following sentences uses the underlined word correctly?
    A. I was depending on her help, but she <u>baled</u> out at the last minute.
    B. He <u>poured</u> over the book as he studied for the exam.
    C. She is <u>adverse</u> to receiving help with the project.
    D. He could not <u>bear</u> to listen to the loud music.

15. Which of the following sentences uses the underlined word correctly?
    A. Her behavior was so <u>bazaar</u> yesterday.
    B. She was accused of conducting <u>illicit</u> financial transactions online.
    C. He gave me a nice <u>complement</u> about my new sweater.
    D. You will need an <u>envelop</u> if you are going to mail that letter.

CITATION AND REFERENCING

Instructions: Answer the following questions on referencing and citation. You may wish to view the Source, Reference, and Citation Guide, provided previously in the study guide, before completing the exercises that follow.

1. As animal rights groups have come more into prominence socially and politically, and people are more and more aware of the suffering of animals, many people question whether using animals in this way is medically reasonable, or whether it is even ethical or moral.

    Which of the following sentences demonstrates the best way to cite the information in the sentence above from a publication entitled *DNA Research*? **(D)**
    - A. It has been questioned whether using animals for medical research is reasonable.
    - B. Recent research indicates that "animal rights groups question whether the suffering of animals for medical reasons is ethical or moral."
    - C. According to *DNA Research,* more and more people are questioning whether using animals for DNA research is "medically reasonable".
    - D. Many people have doubts about whether using animals for DNA research is "medically reasonable, or whether it is even ethical or moral" (*DNA Research*).

2. Which of the following entries from a reading list is in the correct style and format? **(M)**
    - A. Anderson, G. (2015, January 7). Neighborhood decline in American cities. *Society Today,* 125(3), 25-32.
    - B. *Anderson, G.* (2015, January 7). Neighborhood decline in American cities. *Society Today,* 125(3), 25-32.
    - C. *Anderson, G.* (2015, January 7). *Neighborhood decline in American cities. Society Today,* 125(3), 25-32.
    - D. Anderson, G. (2015, January 7). Neighborhood decline in American cities. Society Today, 125(3), 25-32.

3. Which of the following entries from a reading list is in the correct style and format? **(M)**
    - A. *Brown, Mark.* (2012). *Old towns: A study in urban development.* Pittsburg: Authors' Press.
    - B. Brown, Mark. (2012). *Old towns: A study in urban development.* Pittsburg: Authors' Press.
    - C. Brown, Mark. (2012). *Old towns: A study in urban development. Pittsburg: Authors' Press.*
    - D. Brown, Mark. (2012). Old towns: A study in urban development. Pittsburg: Authors' Press.

4. What is the main purpose of reviewing a reading list when conducting research for a term paper or other research project? **(M)**

    - A. to check for plagiarism in the work of others
    - B. to assess the veracity of quotations within an article
    - C. to identify further sources to use in your research
    - D. to determine whether the list of references has been provided in the correct format

5. Smith, C. (2013). *American history in the twenty-first century.* New York: Independent Publishers. The item above is from a list of references. Which of the following is being cited? **(A)**
    - A. a newspaper article
    - B. a magazine article
    - C. an article from a scholarly journal
    - D. a book

WRITING SKILLS EXERCISES

Instructions: Read the early draft of an essay and choose the best answer to the questions that follow.

(1) The theory of multiple intelligences is rapidly replacing the intelligence quotient, also known as IQ.

_____

_____

(3) Many academic administrators also consider the theory of multiple intelligences to be more useful than that of IQ because it measures practical skills such as spatial, visual, and musical ability.

(4) If a person has visual or spatial intelligence, he or she will be good at perceiving visual images. **(5)** To put it another way, people with spatial intelligence will have a knack for interpreting things like maps and charts. **(6)** Verbal or linguistic intelligence is another one of the multiple intelligences, and it includes skills like public speaking or telling stories. **(7)** There is also musical intelligence; so for instance, if a person can sing or play a musical instrument, he or she probably possesses this type of intelligence.

(8) Famous sports personalities have what is known as bodily or kinesthetic intelligence, which means that their skillful in controlling their bodily movements. **(9)** If you ever have the occasion to teach someone with kinesthetic intelligence, you will quickly realize that trying to do so is the ultimate nightmare since sitting in a classroom for extended periods of time is definitely not something these types of learners enjoy.

(10) Howard Gardner devised the system of multiple intelligences, which posited that while most people have one dominant type of intelligence, most of us have more than one type. **(11)** It is because of this plurality, of course, that they are called multiple intelligences. **(12)** The theory of multiple intelligences therefore has implications for teaching and learning.

1. The introduction to the essay above is incomplete. Which sentence below best completes the introduction? **(M)**
   - A. IQ, the intelligence quotient, is used by organizations like Mensa to assess an individual's intellectual ability.
   - B. Recent psychometric research indicates that there has been a movement away from the IQ test, which many believe should only be used as an indication of a person's academic ability.
   - C. Many academic administrators lament that the IQ is going out of fashion.
   - D. The IQ test is still popular in many institutions in the United States.

2. Sentence 3 is reproduced below.
   Many academic administrators also consider the theory of multiple intelligences to be more useful than that of IQ because it measures practical skills such as spatial, visual, and musical ability.
   The student is considering adding this new sentence after sentence 3:
   In fact, a recent survey has revealed that over 75% of the schools in our district are now using placement tests based upon the theory of multiple intelligences.
   Should the student make this addition to the essay? **(D)**
   - A. No, because it repeats ideas that have already been mentioned in the previous sentence.
   - B. No, because it fails precisely to describe how the statistics have been complied and is therefore not based on reliable data.
   - C. Yes, because the statistics in the new sentence support the main idea of the paragraph.
   - D. Yes, because the sentence provides a link to concept of visual and spatial intelligence that is mentioned in the next paragraph.

3. Which is the best version of the underlined portion of sentence 6, reproduced below? **(M)**
Verbal or linguistic intelligence is another one of the multiple intelligences, and <u>it includes skills</u> like public speaking or telling stories.
   A. Leave it as it is now.
   B. they include skills
   C. it included skills
   D. they included skills

4. Which is the best decision regarding the underlined portion of sentence 8, reproduced below? **(M)**
Famous sports personalities have what is known as bodily or kinesthetic intelligence, which means that <u>their skillful in</u> controlling their bodily movements.
   A. Leave it as it is now.
   B. Delete the words "skillful in"
   C. Change the word "their" to "there"
   D. Change the word "their" to "they are"

5. What is the most logical placement for sentence 12, reproduced below? **(D)**
The theory of multiple intelligences therefore has implications for teaching and learning.
   A. Where it is now.
   B. After sentence 1.
   C. After sentence 7.
   D. After sentence 9.

(1) In the Black Hills in the state of South Dakota, four visages protrude from the side of a mountain. **(2)** The faces are those of four United States' presidents: George Washington, Thomas Jefferson, Theodore Roosevelt, and Abraham Lincoln. **(3)** Directed by the Danish-American sculptor John Gutzon Borglum, working on this giant display of outdoor art was a Herculean task that took 14 years to complete.

(4) A South Dakota state historian named Doane Robinson originally conceived of the idea for the memorial sculpture. **(5)** He proposed that the work be dedicated to popular figures who were prominent in the western United States and accordingly suggested statues of western heroes such as Buffalo Bill Cody and Kit Carson. **(6)** Deeming a project dedicated to popular heroes frivolous, Borglum rejected Robinson's proposal. **(7)** It was Borglum's firm conviction that the mountain carving be used to memorialize individuals of national importance.

(8) Mount Rushmore therefore became a memorial dedicated to the four presidents who were considered most pivotal in US history. **(9)** Washington was chosen on the basis of being the first president. Jefferson, who was of course a president, was also instrumental in the writing of the American Declaration of Independence. **(10)** Lincoln was selected on the basis of the mettle he demonstrated during the American Civil War and Roosevelt for his development of Square Deal policy, as well as for being a proponent of the construction of the Panama Canal.

(11) Commencing with Washington's head first, Borglum quickly realized that it would be best to work on only one head at a time in order to make each one compatible with its surroundings. **(12)** To help visualize the final outcome. **(13)** He fashioned a 1.5-meter high plaster model on a scale of 1 to 12.

(14) Work on the venture began in 1927 and was completed in 1941. **(15)** The financing required in order to create such a massive monument surpassed all expectation. **(16)** The total cost of the project was nearly one million dollars. **(17)** The financing for the project was provided mostly from national government funds and also from charitable donations from magnanimous members of the public.

6. Which is the best decision regarding the underlined portion of sentence 3, reproduced below? **(M)**
   Directed by the Danish-American sculptor John Gutzon Borglum, working on this giant display of outdoor art was a Herculean task that took 14 years to complete.
   A. Leave it as it is now.
   B. Delete the words "giant display of"
   C. Change the word "working" to "having worked"
   D. Change the word "working" to "the work"

7. Which version of the underlined portion of sentence 7, reproduced below, provides the most effective contrast to the point mentioned in the previous sentence? **(A)**
   It was Borglum's firm conviction that the mountain carving be used to memorialize individuals of national importance.
   A. Leave it as it is now.
   B. national—not heroic—importance
   C. national, rather than regional, importance
   D. national, not western, importance

8. Which version of the underlined portion of sentence 8, reproduced below, provides the most effective topic sentence for paragraph 3? **(D)**
   Mount Rushmore therefore became a memorial dedicated to the four presidents who were considered most pivotal in US history.
   A. Leave it as it is now.
   B. national memorial dedicated
   C. national memorial, dedicated
   D. memorial, dedicated

9. Which choice most effectively combines sentences 12 and 13, reproduced below, at the underlined portion? **(M)**
   To help visualize the final outcome. He fashioned a 1.5 meter high plaster model on a scale of 1 to 12.
   A. Leave it as it is now.
   B. outcome—he fashioned
   C. outcome; He fashioned
   D. outcome, he fashioned

10. Sentence 16 is reproduced below.
    The total cost of the project was nearly one million dollars.
    The student is considering adding the following text at the end of the sentence:
    which would be worth over seventy million dollars today
    Should the student make this addition there? **(D)**
    A. No, because it makes the sentence unnecessarily verbose.
    B. No, because it breaks up the chronological flow of the paragraph.
    C. Yes, because it emphasizes how expensive the project was.
    D. Yes, because most of the financing was provided by members of the public.

(1) An efficient electron microscope can magnify an object by more than one million times its original size. **(2)** This innovation has thereby allowed scientists to study the precise molecules that constitute human life.

(3) The electron microscope functions by emitting a stream of electrons from a gun-type instrument, which is similar to the apparatus used in an old-fashioned television tube. **(4)** The electrons emitted from the instrument passes through an advanced electronic field that is accelerated to millions of volts in certain cases. **(5)** Before traveling through a vacuum in order to remove oxygen molecules, the electrons are focused into a beam by way of magnetic coils.

(6) Invisible to the naked eye, electron beams can nevertheless be projected onto a florescent screen. **(7)** When striking the screen, the electrons glow and can even be recorded on film. **(8)** Old-fashioned cameras also used film to capture images.

(9) In the transmission electron microscope, which is used to study cells or tissues, the beam passes through a thin slice of the specimen that is being studied. **(10)** On the other hand, in the scanning electron microscope, utilized for tasks such as examining bullets and fibers. **(11)** The beam is reflected. **(12)** This reflection creates a picture of the specimen line by line.

11. Which version of the underlined portion of sentence 1, reproduced below, provides the most effective introduction to the essay? **(D)**
    An efficient electron microscope <u>can magnify an object by more than one million times its original size</u>.
    A. Leave it as it is now.
    B. can be used for many important scientific tasks
    C. has revolutionized scientific study
    D. emits beams or electrons in order to function

12. Which is the best version of the underlined portion of sentence 4, reproduced below? **(M)**
    The electrons <u>emitted from the instrument passes</u> through an advanced electronic field that is accelerated to millions of volts in certain cases.
    A. Leave it as it is now.
    B. emitted from the instrument pass
    C. emitting from the instrument passes
    D. being emitted from the instrument passes

13. Which sentence blurs the focus of the essay and should therefore be deleted? **(A)**
    A. Sentence 3
    B. Sentence 5
    C. Sentence 8
    D. Sentence 9

14. Which is the best decision regarding the underlined portion of sentence 9, reproduced below? **(D)**
    In the transmission electron microscope, which is used to study cells or tissues, the beam passes through a thin slice of the <u>specimen that is being studied</u>.
    A. Leave it as it is now.
    B. Change "that is being studied" to "that was being studied"
    C. Change "that is being studied" to "that scientists study"
    D. Change "that is being studied" to "that scientists are studying"

15. Identify the two sentences below that create the best conclusion to this essay. **(D)**
    A. In spite of their different functions, both types of microscopes have proved useful for modern society.
    B. In television shows like CSI, we often see scientists using microscopes to examine specimens.
    C. The use of microscopes is therefore likely to become of increasing importance in the future.
    D. Some members of the scientific community find fault with both types of microscopes.
    E. Old-fashioned devices like the X-ray and "box-style" TV's will soon completely disappear.

(1) The tradition of music in the western world originated in the genre of chanting. **(2)** Chant, a monophonic form of music, was the dominant mode of music prior to the thirteenth century. **(3)** Monophonic music consists of only one sound or voice that combines various notes in a series. **(4)** Monophonic is a word that is Greek in origin. **(5)** Polyphonic music appeared in the fifteenth century during the early Renaissance period, and it combines the notes from the different sources together simultaneously. **(6)** As polyphony developed, musical traditions began to change, and this meant that music began to rely on a greater range of voices.

(7) In contrast to monophonic music, polyphonic music consists of more than one voice or instrument. **(8)** During the sixteenth century, there was an attempt to return to the tradition of Greek drama. **(9)** This had an extremely positive impact on the opera. **(10)** As a result, the opera expanded during the seventeenth century to include oratorios, which are sung musical compositions on a particular subject. **(11)** This phenomenon occurred in the opera, and so, the opera, in turn, influenced the musical style of the seventeenth century.

(12) The seventeenth century also witnessed the proliferation of musical instruments. **(13)** Musical compositions and arrangements for keyboard instruments, such as the piano and organ, thrived during this period.

(14) The eighteenth century was marked by the development of baroque music. **(15)** This century was dominated by two German-born geniuses, Bach and Handel. **(16)** These two composers wrote music in almost every genre, including opera and oratorio music.

(17) Beethoven is the crucial link between the classical and romantic periods. **(18)** To his compositions, he added deeper texture, meaning the depth and breadth of different types of musical sound. **(19)** For this reason, Beethoven's music is commonly regarded as establishing the end of the classical period.

16. Which sentence is least relevant to the introduction? **(D)**
    A. Sentence 3
    B. Sentence 4
    C. Sentence 5
    D. Sentence 6

17. What is the most logical placement for sentence 7, reproduced below? **(D)**
    In contrast to monophonic music, polyphonic music consists of more than one voice or instrument.
    A. Where it is now.
    B. After sentence 3
    C. After sentence 4
    D. After sentence 5

18. Which is the best decision regarding sentence 11, reproduced below? **(M)**
    This phenomenon occurred in the opera, and so, the opera, in turn, influenced the musical style of the seventeenth century.
    A. Leave it as it is now.
    B. Delete the phrase "so, the opera, in turn,"
    C. Delete the phrase "in turn,"
    D. Delete the entire sentence from the essay.

19. Which is the best version of the underlined portion of sentence 15, reproduced below? **(M)**
    This century was dominated by two German-born <u>geniuses, Bach</u> and Handel.
    A. Leave it as it is now.
    B. geniuses: Bach
    C. geniuses; Bach
    D. geniuses who were Bach

20. Which two of the sentences below would provide the best conclusion to the essay? **(A)**
    A. Students of music are therefore likely to learn all about these different musical periods during their studies.
    B. Classical music has continued to endure throughout the centuries.
    C. Classical music has an effect on musicians from the Beatles to current-day artists.
    D. Indeed, the different styles of classical music are still enjoyed by many around the word today.
    E. However, many people regard classical music as dry and boring.

(1) Like many of my colleagues who decided to embark on a career in teaching, I was positively influenced by a teacher who helped me through some difficult personal struggles. **(2)** The support and concern that this teacher gave me was significant in my own decision to enter the teaching profession.

(3) Having had very prominent buck teeth until undergoing orthodontic work in my late teens, I was dubbed "Bugs Bunny" by my classmates in second grade. **(4)** This nickname made me even more awkward and shy than before, and self-confidence began to illude me. **(5)** I coped with the problem the best I could have at that age: by retreating into my own world of books and reading.

(6) Fortunately, I had one close friend throughout grades 3, 4, and 5. **(7)** She shared my affinity with reading, and we often exchanged books with each other during summer vacations. **(8)** Without even realizing it, I was quickly becoming a very proficient reader at a young age.

(9) Upon returning to school at the beginning of the sixth grade, my entire self-concept began to change. **(10)** At the start of the year, I found out who I would be having as my home room and reading teacher—Mrs. Shelley. **(11)** I had heard so many nice things about her and her classes, and she always had a warm smile and time to talk to everyone she met.

(12) Mrs. Shelly often complimented me in private after class about my reading skills. **(13)** Her kindness and sincerity demonstrated to me at an early age the true essence of being a good teacher. **(14)** I knew that other students didn't like to read as much as I did. **(15)** Soon my classmates' views of me just didn't matter anymore. **(16)** I had found something that was important to me: the desire to help other people the way that Mrs. Shelley had helped me. **(17)** This impulse remained with me throughout middle school and high school, and it was a major factor in my own decision to become a teacher.

21. Which is the best version of the underlined portion of sentence 2, reproduced below? **(M)**
    The support and concern that this teacher gave me <u>was significant</u> in my own decision to enter the teaching profession.
    A. Leave it as it is now.
    B. were significant
    C. was being significant
    D. had been significant

22. Which is the best version of the underlined portion of sentence 4, reproduced below? **(D)**
    This nickname made me even more awkward and shy than before, and self-confidence began to illude me.
    A. Leave it as it is now.
    B. allude
    C. allure
    D. elude

23. Sentence 8 is reproduced below.
    Without even realizing it, I was quickly becoming a very proficient reader at a young age.
    The student is considering adding the following text at the end of the sentence:
    , but I remained shy and lacking in self-confidence
    Should the student make this addition there? **(A)**
    A. No, because the student already mentions his lack of self-confidence in the previous paragraph.
    B. No, because these words will break the logical flow of the essay.
    C. Yes, because this paragraph in the essay is describing how the student continued to feel as he grew up.
    D. Yes, because these events are the same as those in the sixth grade, which the student describes in the next paragraph.

24. Which is the best decision regarding the underlined portion of sentence 10, reproduced below? **(D)**
    At the start of the year, I found out who I would be having as my home room and reading teacher—Mrs. Shelley.
    A. Leave it as it is now.
    B. Delete the dash.
    C. Use a comma instead of a dash.
    D. Delete the phrase from the sentence.

25. Which sentence blurs the focus of the last paragraph and should therefore be deleted? **(A)**
    A. Sentence 12
    B. Sentence 13
    C. Sentence 14
    D. Sentence 15

ANSWERS AND EXPLANATIONS

READING PRACTICE TEST 1

1. The correct answer is D. Damaged packages should be placed into container E, regardless of their weight. This package has been erroneously placed into container B. The final paragraph states that if an item is placed into the wrong sorting container, there will be a delay of 5 days.

2. The correct answer is B. Container D is for all packages that are 80 ounces or more in weight.

3. The correct answer is C. The first paragraph states: "We have placed a special staging station in the middle of the room."

4. The correct answer is D. Failing to pre-heat the oven will result in the cake being dry and dense. Paragraph 1 of the passage states: "For a moist and fluffy cake, you should first of all pre-heat the oven to 350 degrees." The opposite of moist is dry, and the opposite of fluffy is dense.

5. The correct answer is B. Be careful with questions like this because the sentences in the passage may not be given in sequential order. Notice the sentence: "Check that your bowl is big enough before you put anything in it." This indicates that you must check the size of the bowl after preparing the pan and before mixing the ingredients.

6. The correct answer is D. The second locomotive that Stephenson invented was an improvement on his first because it ran with greater force and speed. The last sentence of the article states that "Stephenson's second train was even faster and more powerful than his first one."

7. The correct answer is C. The first sentence states: "The world's first public railway was very modern and useful." The words "modern" and "useful" are roughly similar to "important and practical."

8. The correct answers are A and B. These sentences support the answer because they mention the two purposes of the train. So, they explain why the train was important and practical.

9. The correct answer is 6. Paragraph 4 describes the improved train, and row 6 is the only row of the chart that gives information on the new train. The other rows of the chart give information on the first train.

10. The correct answer is B. The author's purpose is clearly stated in the first sentence of the article: "Jean Piaget is one of the most well-known theorists in child development and educational psychology, and the scholastic community still discusses his principles today."

11. The correct answers are B and C. These are two of the most significant aspects of Piaget's research. You may be tempted to choose answer A, but this gives background about Piaget, rather than focusing on an aspect of his work. The other answer choices are too specific.

12. The correct answer is D. Paragraph 1 states: "Piaget determined that younger children responded to research questions differently than older children. His conclusion was that different responses occurred not because younger children were less intelligent, but because they were at a lower level of biological development." In other words, he linked their intellectual ability to their biological development.

13. The correct answer is D. Answer A is true because the first sentence of paragraph 2 talks about Piaget's work as a biologist. Answer B is true since the second sentence of paragraph 2 describes Piaget's discovery of mental schemes. Answer C is true because the last sentence of paragraph 2 provides details about environmental adaptation. The paragraph does not state that Piaget was the first researcher in this field, so choice D is not true.

14. The correct answer is A. The second sentence of paragraph 5 states that the sensorimotor stage is the first stage.

15. The correct answer is B. "Exemplify" means to give an example. Bottle feeding is given as an example in paragraph 4 because this idea is introduced by using the phrase "for example."

16. The correct answer is D. Paragraph 5 mentions that in this stage "intelligence is demonstrated in the manner in which the infant interacts physically with the world." The words "mobility" and "motor activity" in this paragraph also express the idea of physical movement. Note that "cognitive" means intellectual.

17. The correct answer is A. Paragraph 7 mentions that "logical and systematic thought processes appear" during the concrete operational stage. Since these skills appear during the concrete operational stage, they don't exist prior to this time.

18. The correct answer is C. The words "inflexible" and "illogical" are synonymous to "rigid and unsystematic."

19. The correct answer is A. It can be inferred that patients today would most likely respond to treatments of the past with fear. We can assume that burning the skin was feared because it is described as a "so-called" treatment. In addition, the second sentence of paragraph 2 implies that these treatments were inhumane.

20. The correct answer is C. The primary purpose of the article is to discuss Pasteur's discovery of the rabies vaccine. Paragraph 1 focuses on Pasteur's research on rabies. Paragraphs 2 and 3 describe how the discovery of the rabies vaccine was made.

21. The correct answer is B. The article suggests that the discovery of the rabies vaccine was significant because it helped many people avoid physical suffering and death. We know this because paragraph 1 explains that patients with rabies would suffer from "convulsions and delirium, and it would be too late to administer any remedy."

22. The correct answer is A. The phrase "too late to administer any remedy" indicates that the patient would die from the infection.

23. The correct answer is B. The third paragraph states: "the vaccine is administered before the microorganism is encountered and stimulates the immune system to recognize and fight off any future exposure to the organism." In other words, the steps are (1) the vaccine is administered; (2) the vaccine stimulates the immune system to recognize and fight off any future exposure to the organism; (3) the patient is protected against the contagion.

24. The correct answer is B. "These differences" refers to the phrase "variations in soil composition" which is mentioned in the previous sentence in paragraph 4.

25. The correct answer is D. Paragraph 2 states: "A logical locality to begin searching is one near sites in which artifacts have been found previously."

26. The correct answer is D. The meaning of this word is revealed in the next sentence in paragraph 5: "the mechanism goes back and forth in this way . . ."

27. The correct answer is A. Sentence 2 of paragraph 6 states that cataloging "can certainly be tedious; yet, it is one that is critical in order to account for each and every item properly." The phrase "account for" means to be sure that every item is present, or stated conversely, to be sure that no item is missing.

28. The correct answer is C. The last sentence of paragraph 7 states: "Unfortunately, as a consequence, the misapprehension that the origins of homo sapiens were European began to take shape both in the archeological and wider communities."

29. The correct answer is C. The word "unfortunately" makes it clear that this action is regrettable. The words "misunderstanding" and "misapprehension" are synonyms. The phrase "wider communities" means culturally.

30. The correct answer is A. The last paragraph states: "By the middle of the 1900's, [. . .] there was a surge in artifacts excavated from African and Asian localities." Since there was a surge or sudden increase in the discovery of artifacts from Asia and Africa around the 1950's, we can conclude that there were few archeological findings from these areas previously.

31. The correct answer is C. The article discusses the three main ideas stated in choice C. The following statement in choices A and D is false according to the article: "The European archeological discoveries of the 1800s should be disregarded." The other ideas mentioned in choices A, B, and D are true according to the article, but they are specific points, not main ideas. Artifact interpretation and Darwinian theory are archeological developments, not archeological field methods.

32. The correct answer is B. The use of quotations in the article suggests that the followers of Noh are traditional, discerning, and serious. Paragraphs 1 and 2 use quotation marks when they state that Noh is for the "discriminating Japanese aristocracy" and that it depicts a "solemn act." The word "aristocracy" indicates that the dance is traditional in nature. "Discriminating" means "discerning," and "solemn" means "serious."

33. The correct answer is A. The fourth paragraph implies that Japanese audiences today would respond to Kabuki theater with admiration. The last sentence of the fourth paragraph states: "Because of its appeal to the general populace, Kabuki theater remains as fascinating and exotic as it has always been." We can surmise that people probably admire something that fascinates them.

34. The correct answer is D. Followers of Noh and followers of Kabuki would probably agree that Japanese theater is an important and interesting aspect of Japanese culture. The first sentence of the article explains that these forms of theater "have emerged from Japanese culture." Since an article has been devoted to this topic, we can assume that followers consider the topic to be an important and interesting aspect of the Japanese culture.

35. The correct answer is B. The primary purpose of the first two paragraphs is to explain the basic tenets of Marxism. We know this because the second sentence begins with the phrase "according to Marxism." Answer A is too general, and answers C and D are mentioned later in the article.

36. The correct answer is D. The first two paragraphs give the background to the topic in a general way, and paragraphs 3 and 4 provide specific details about the topic. You may be tempted to choose answer C, but the criticism is only one aspect of the information provided in paragraph 4.

37. The correct answer is A. The writer mentions the "huge impact" that these writings have had on culture and politics in the last sentence in order to juxtapose this impact to Marx's failure to include pragmatic instructions in his work. We know that the author is making a juxtaposition or comparison because the sentence begins with the word "yet."

38. The correct answer is A. The narrator is being sarcastic. He is stranded and alone, so there is no one over whom he can reign.

39. The correct answer is D. "Reproach" means scold; "unthankful temper" means not appreciating what one has; "solitary condition" means loneliness, and the utterance "what I would give to be on shore there again" means that he wants to go back to the island.

40. The correct answer is A. The statement "we never see the true state of our condition till it is illustrated to us by its contraries" would be expressed in present-day English as "you don't know what you've got until it's gone."

READING PRACTICE TEST 2

1. The correct answer is A. The theory described in paragraph 2 appeared in the first century. It is also described as "unformulated." For these reasons, we know that the theory was newly formed.

2. The correct answer is C. "Compatriot" means a person who has the same nationality as someone else. At the beginning of paragraph 2, Ptolemy is described as "another Greek scientist."

3. The correct answer is C. "Flash of inspiration" means that a single event suddenly causes a positive outcome. It is the opposite of the phrase "slowly developed over time." So, the law of gravity was created slowly.

4. The correct answer is B. The author's attitude is expressed in paragraph 5.

5. The correct answer is A. The word "importance" in the following sentence shows that an attitude or opinion is being expressed: "Newton's study was of great importance for the scientific community and for society as a whole."

6. The correct answer is B. "Reservation" means confusion or doubt. It is close in meaning to the word "perplexed" and the phrase "unable adequately to explain."

7. The correct answer is A. Paragraph 7 states that "Einstein asserted that the paths of objects in motion can sometimes . . . change direction . . . as a result of the curvature of space time."

8. The correct answer is B. Paragraph 7 states that Einstein's work was "revolutionary" and that it has been "unequivocally supported." Both of these statements describe positive reactions.

9. The correct answer is D. The grammatical subject of this clause in the sentence is "contribution." "Benefit" and "contribution" are near synonyms.

10. The correct answer is D. Paragraph 4 states that "Recently, cultural and critical theorists have joined in the economic debate", so A is correct. Paragraph 4 also states that "various forms of media promote the mechanisms of economic manipulation and oppression," so B is correct. Finally, paragraph 4 states that "those of lower socio-economic class . . . view themselves as . . . powerless victims." So C is also correct.

11. The correct answer is B. "Poorer countries" is synonymous with "less economically advanced." "Peripheral" is similar in meaning to "irrelevant." Finally, "policy" is similar in meaning to "protocol."

12. The correct answer is C. The economic effects of social inequality is the main theme of this reading article. So, the author wants to illustrate the main theme. The answer B is too strongly-worded and emphatic, and answers A are D are too specific.

13. The correct answer is A. This is expressed clearly in paragraphs 4 and 5. Note that answer choice D exaggerates the consequence of early death.

14. The correct answer is C. Paragraph 5 explains that these personal consequences affect tastes, perceptions, and emotions.

15. The correct answer is C. The article is speaking about the harm caused to low-paid people. Answers A, B, and D contain words with positive connotations.

16. The correct answer is C. The word "conversely" at the beginning of paragraph 7 indicates that there is a dispute or disagreement.

17. The correct answer is C. Paragraph 1 states the main idea of these paragraphs: "movie stars who regularly smoke in films are influencing young people to smoke cigarettes."

18. The correct answer is C. Paragraph 4 states: "The WHO survey found that 76% of the most popular films produced worldwide within the last ten years showed some form of tobacco use." You may be tempted to choose answer A. However, 65% represents the number of actors who are portrayed smoking in movies.

19. The correct answer is B. In paragraph 4, we read that "the WHO's World No Tobacco Day focuses on how the fashion and film industries glamorize cigarettes."

20. The correct answer is D. The information about the WHO can be found in paragraph 4.

21. The correct answer is D. The last sentence of paragraph 4 gives the most significant idea of the paragraph: "This research shows a clear relation between on-screen tobacco use by movie stars and higher levels of beginning to smoke by the teenagers who admire them." The other answers provide information that merely supports the main, significant finding.

22. The correct answers are B, C, and E. The information to support these answers is in paragraphs 4, 7, and 8.

23. The correct answer is A. We can understand that paragraph 8 is providing statistics because of the number of percentages and other figures it includes.

24. The correct answer is B. According to Dr. Edward Adams, the increase in experimental smoking is accompanied by an increase in that of regular smoking. Paragraph 9 states: "The rise in those experimenting with smoking has been matched by an increase in regular smokers as well."

25. The correct answer is B. Paragraph 10 points out that children who "showed signs of being hooked only had an average of two cigarettes a week. Some of these kids were hooked within a few days of starting to smoke."

26. The correct answer is C. Paragraph 10 states: "His team suggested that brains of adolescents, because they were still growing, were more vulnerable to addiction. The effect of tobacco might be stronger and longer lasting than in adults."

27. The correct answer is A. In the first paragraph, the author suggests that our mental and physiological sense of time is appropriate. The author explains that all human beings have this sense of time. The author does not criticize this behavior, but rather, provides factual information about the topic. From the tone of the article, we can therefore surmise that that author views this behavior as appropriate.

28. The correct answer is B. In the fourth paragraph, the phrase "these cycles" refers to circadian rhythms. The two previous sentences state: "Circadian rhythms help to explain the "lark vs. owl" hypothesis. Larks are those who quite rightly prefer to rise early in the morning and go to bed early, while owls are those who feel at their best at night and stay up too late." Larks and owls are given as an

example, so the phrase "these rhythms" refers back to the subject of circadian rhythms in the previous sentence.

29. The correct answer is A. The author's attitude toward owls in the "lark vs. owl" hypothesis can best be described as one of disapproval. The author says that larks "quite rightly prefer to rise early in the morning," but owls "stay up too late."

30. The correct answer is B. The phrase "stay up too late" shows that the author disapproves of the owl's behavior.

31. The correct answer is C. The sentence before this one states that "a funnel is produced that extends from the cloud above it to the earth below." So, we know that the funnel hangs from the cloud.

32. The correct answer is D. Paragraph 4 states that tornadoes cause 70 deaths each year in the US. It also states that tornadoes "usually occur between 3:00 PM and 9:00 PM." Finally, the paragraph mentions that tornadoes are most common during the summer. Wind speed is not mentioned until paragraph 5.

33. The correct answer is C. "Myriad" means very many or an innumerable amount.

34. The correct answer is A. The author's purpose is stated in the topic sentence, which is the first sentence of the paragraph.

35. The correct answer is A. The author's purpose is stated in this sentence: "Tornadoes are normally classified as weak, strong, or violent."

36. The correct answer is B. Paragraph 6 states: "For example, some people hold the view that tornadoes cannot occur over oceans, lakes, or rivers. However, waterspouts, tornadoes that develop over bodies of water, can in many cases cause major damage to coastal areas as they move onshore." So, we can see that this is an example of misinformation. The idea of misinformation is also mentioned in paragraph 1, which states that "very few people actually understand how these weather events occur."

37. The correct answer is D. Paragraph 6 talks about myths and misconceptions. Both of these words mean that people do not possess factual information about a certain topic.

38. The correct answer is A. This sentence talks about "another myth."

39. The correct answer is D. The article mainly discusses the loss of life and property caused by tornadoes. Answer choices A, B, and C are specific points from the article.

40. The correct answer is A. The article mentions the two ideas summarized in answer choice A. The other information in answer choices B, C, and D is mentioned in the article as specific points, not main ideas.

READING PRACTICE TEST 3

1. The correct answer is C. The best title for the article is "The Changing Face of Tourism." The first sentence of the article states: "Adventurers, fieldwork assistants, and volunteers are gradually replacing tourists." This sentence introduces the idea of changes to tourism, and these changes are explained in depth in the article.

2. The correct answer is C. The title "The Changing Face of Tourism" relates to the author's assertion that people will travel, but perhaps secretly or on a different kind of vacation. Answer choice C sums up this idea.

3. The correct answer is B. The word "clandestine" has the same meaning as "secret." We know that tourism has become a secret activity because paragraph 1 states that traveling for enjoyment will become a "frowned-upon activity [. . . that] no one will admit to."

4. The correct answer is C. The author does not discuss the reasons why flights became inexpensive. The article merely states that "the advent of relatively less expensive accommodation and flights has meant that tourism can finally be enjoyed by the majority."

5. The correct answer is C. "Emulate" means to imitate. The example in paragraph 8 points out that *Global Adventure* magazine treats charitable expeditions and vacations "as if the two things are one and the same."

6. The correct answer is D. The words "these notions" refer to the viewpoints that express disdain for tourism. We know this because the previous sentence in the article expresses the belief that tourism "must be stopped at any price."

7. The correct answer is C. The author mentions "cultural experiences", "expeditions" or "projects" in paragraph 7 of the article to illustrate how tourism has been re-branded. The last sentence of paragraph 7 states that "re-branding tourism in this way gives freedom to travelers, as well as restrictions." Paragraph 6 also mentions that tourism "has been renamed."

8. The correct answer is A. The author expresses regret towards the past effects of tourism on the environment in the last paragraph.

9. The correct answer is B. We can assume that the author feels regret because the last paragraph claims that "all types of tourism should be responsible towards and respectful of environmental and human resources." He has previously mentioned in the article that this has not always been the case.

10. The correct answer is C. The author's main purpose in the article is to enumerate the reasons for health inequalities, particularly in children, and to allude to some possible courses of action. Paragraph 4 mentions the solution of school breakfast and dinner programs. Paragraph 5 asserts that the "authorities [need] to address nutrition as one of the worst symptoms of child poverty." Paragraph 6 claims that more government funds should be allocated to preventing cigarette sales to children. Finally, the last paragraph proposes "the allocation of governmental funds to nutrition and effective education."

11. The correct answer is D. The author mentions child poverty and poor health, as well as potential solutions to these problems, in several paragraphs in the article. This is also evident in the final paragraph of the article, which talks about improving children's opportunities.

12. The correct answer is B. Paragraph 1 does not state that alcohol consumption has risen across many age groups in the last ten years. It merely points out that that there has been an increase in the consumption of alcoholic beverages by a particular group, namely, among the 11-to-15-year-old age group.

13. The correct answer is A. The word "they" refers to countries that have established school breakfasts. The previous sentence in paragraph 5 mentions that "some countries have developed programs for nutritious school breakfasts and dinners."

14. The correct answer is B. The best explanation is as follows: "Poor children do not start the day with a good meal and cannot learn well as a result, so it is of the utmost importance for the government to improve child poverty and child nutrition" The phrase "poor children do not start the day with a good meal and cannot learn well as a result" means the same as "disadvantaged children in many areas still do not get a nourishing breakfast and the effectiveness of their education is jeopardized as a result." The phrase "so it is of the utmost importance for the government to improve child poverty and child nutrition" means

the same thing as "there remains a clear need for the authorities to address nutrition as one of the worst symptoms of child poverty."

15. The correct answer is D. The author discusses smoking in paragraph 6 in order to expand on another aspect of poor health in children. We know this because the first sentence of paragraph 6 points out that "smoking also greatly damages the health of children and increases childhood mortality rates."

16. The correct answer is A. Based on paragraph 7, we can infer that the government is reluctant to criticize the practices of big businesses because it is loath to lose the monetary support that large beverage companies have to offer. "Loath" means "unwilling or reluctant."

17. The correct answer is D. This sentence mentions "big businesses like Anheuser-Busch," which is a large beverage company.

18. The correct answer is D. The relationship between the goals of improved opportunities for children and the problems of child poverty and ill health is best described as follows: The achievement of the goal of the reduction of child poverty would improve child health and increase the opportunities of children to some extent, but it would not entirely eradicate the problem. Paragraph 8 states that "while these goals are related, it would be foolish to believe that the reduction of child poverty would automatically improve children's nutrition and reduce their smoking and drinking."

19. The correct answer is C. The word "catalyst" in this article is closest in meaning to "reason." We know that immigration is the reason because paragraph 1 states that the population has risen because immigration has increased.

20. The correct answer is B. The words "this steady influx" refer to the constant increase in people coming to the country for the first time. The previous paragraph describes how net inward migration increased during the study.

21. The correct answer is A. The most notable change to the population in the last one hundred years was the three-fold increase in the size of the population. Paragraph 3 clarifies that "notably, the population tripled from almost 76 million at the beginning of the twentieth century to nearly 281 million at the start of the twenty-first century."

22. The correct answer is A. The author mentions the changes to the populations of Florida and Arizona to point out that new residents are continually moving to these states." Paragraph 3 mentions that "Florida and Arizona had the fastest-growing populations during the period of the study."

23. The correct answer is C. The phrase "lion's share of" is closest in meaning to "majority of." The sentence is talking about an increase in consumer credit, so we can surmise that credit cards are the primary cause for this phenomenon.

24. The correct answer is B. A possible interpretation is that the divorce rate went down because fewer people got married during the period of the study. The author's use of the word "concurrent" emphasizes that the decline in the marriage rate and the decrease in the divorce rate occurred at the same time.

25. The correct answer is C. The author suggests that women are more likely to live alone after losing a life partner than men are. This idea is mentioned at the end of paragraph 4.

26. The correct answer is B. Paragraph 4 points out that "older females were far more likely to live alone than were men." We can infer that one of the primary reasons for living alone is losing one's life partner through death or breakup.

27. The correct answer is A. Paragraphs 1 and 2 talk about how the population has increased as a result of immigration. Paragraphs 3 and 4 discuss notable changes in the concentration of the population in certain states and geographic regions, and paragraph 5 describes the way in which the distribution of income has become increasingly skewed in favor of the rich.

28. The correct answer is D. The concept of synchronous rotation, as it is defined in the article, provides the most likely explanation for the situation in which a telecommunications satellite is always in the same position above a certain city on Earth. This is similar to the way in which the same hemisphere of the Moon always faces the Earth because the paths of the two objects are in sync.

29. The correct answer is D. Point 5 in paragraph 3 states that the last step in lunar evolution was "the cessation of volcanic activity followed by gradual internal cooling." So, we can conclude that after lunar evolution, the temperature of the internal core of the Moon was lower than it was previously.

30. The correct answer is A. An analysis revealing that there are no geological similarities between samples of material from the surface of the Moon and material from the Earth's crust would tend to disprove the hypothesis that the Moon grew out of debris that was dislodged from the Earth's crust. If we assume that the Moon grew out of material from the Earth, we would expect to see some geological similarities.

31. The correct answer is A. The narrator states in paragraph 2 that he needs to spend the autumn "economically," so the reader can surmise that he is having financial problems. Note that the narrator mentions that he is "out of spirits," but this condition is not as serious as suffering from depression.

32. The correct answer is C. The narrator says: "It was one of the two evenings in every week which I was accustomed to spend with my mother and my sister." The word "accustomed" indicates that a routine is being described.

33. The correct answer is B. The doorman would have been the servant who welcomed visitors at the front door of the house.

34. The correct answer is D. "Collegial" means acting like colleagues, or people who work in the same profession. Paragraph 5 of the text explains that Professor Pesca and the narrator met when they were teachers, so the two characters would have been colleagues.

35. The correct answer is C. The last paragraph tells us that swimming was one of the "manly exercises which the Professor believed that he could learn impromptu." The word "impromptu" means "on the spot" or "without previous practice or experience."

36. The correct answer is C. The description moves from the roads, to the garden, and then to the house. In other words, the description moves from the outdoors to the house itself, so the bartonwalls are probably a part of the house.

37. The correct answer is D. Paragraph 1 mentions that it is after dusk and that it was nighttime. We also know from paragraph 1 that Clare was restless and that he had gone out.

38. The correct answer is A. "Mutual bearing" means how they interact with each other. "Third parties" is a formal way of saying "other people."

39. The correct answer is C. We know that the story takes place in a dairy farm because Clare confesses that he has fallen in love with a milkmaid at the end of paragraph 3.

40. The correct answer is D. In the next sentence of the paragraph, the narrator tells us that "Tess was no insignificant creature to toy with and dismiss; but a woman living her precious life—a life which, to herself who endured or enjoyed it, possessed as great a dimension as the life of the mightiest to himself." This sentence describes both the positive and negative experiences in Tess's life. It implies that Clare needs to respect Tess when it states that she "was no insignificant creature to toy with and dismiss."

READING PRACTICE TEST 4

1. The correct answer is C. The main problem that this text addresses is that new small businesses lack the money they need to devote to product and technology development. The main idea of the text is expressed in the thesis statement, which is the last sentence of paragraph 1: "And even if a business is already established in the market, still, it will need money to invest in new product and technology development." Answers A and B are not supported by the text. Answer D is a specific point, not the main idea.

2. The correct answer is A. This is the only answer choice that addresses the problems business have. The other answer choices mention solutions.

3. The correct answer is B. The idea that businesses will certainly fail without borrowing money is the converse of the notion that businesses must seek financing to expand.

4. The correct answer is D. The author mentions both advantages and disadvantages in paragraph 5. The advantage is getting the money. The disadvantage is having to do the paperwork. You may be tempted to choose answer C; however, this statement is too strongly worded.

5. The correct answer is C. The best support for Part A is: "Even if it requires a heavy burden in terms of paperwork, the benefit of the support obtained will far outweigh the bureaucratic inconvenience." The word "support" is synonymous with advantages, while the word "burden" is synonymous with disadvantages.

6. The correct answer is C. The paraphrase "That is why the government is willing to help those kinds of businesses" comes closes in meaning to "That is the unstated subtext of this program" from paragraph 6. You know that "unstated subtext" means a hidden reason for doing something, so you may be tempted to choose answer B, but this is a trap because the government only wishes to obscure the reasons for their provision of funding for technological acvancement, rather than obscuring the reasons for technological advancement per se.

7. The correct answer is A. Paragraphs 6 and 7 suggest that business development improves the national economy. These paragraphs talk about businesses evolving and progressing through innovation and technology.

8. The correct answer is B. The following sentence mentions the improvement to the national economy: "By doing so, the government believes that ideas like these can, likewise, help them develop and expand the U.S. economy." The words "develop" and "expand" are synonymous with making an improvement.

9. The correct answer is C. The SBIR provides financial support to certain small businesses, particularly those wishing to make innovations in technology. You may be tempted to choose answer choice B. However, the article does not imply that businesses must change their products just in order to enter the technology sector. The article implies that the businesses will already be in the technology sector.

10. The correct answer is B. This is the only answer choice that mentions improvements in research and development, which relates back to the purpose of the SBIR.

11. The correct answer is C. The passage uses phrases like "the response . . . is mixed," "many still resist," and "legally possible" to describe these debates.

12. The correct answer is D. The article discusses the debates surrounding these forms of genetic engineering: embryonic stem cell cloning, In Vitro Fertilization, screening unborn children, the human genome project, and human egg donation. It describes the discussions surrounding these techniques, rather than just summarizing them.

13. The correct answer is A. The idea of "designer babies" is one of the biggest controversies mentioned in the article. This issue is discussed in paragraphs 3, 4, and 5.

14. The correct answer is D. Paragraph 2 explains that "If embryonic stem cells, which can turn into any type of tissue, were harvested from the early-stage embryo they could be used to regenerate damaged tissue which is genetically matched to a patient. This would avoid immune rejection." Answer choice A is incorrect because the embryos are not used directly as transplants; they only help to reproduce the tissue.

15. The correct answer is C. This is the only answer choice that mentions tissue rejection.

16. The correct answer is B. Paragraph 6 states: "Fears are that cloning techniques will be taken even further and used to select personality traits in the unborn child, from their hair or eye color, to their ability to perform well in sports or exams." The fear that the technique "will be taken even further" means that people are afraid it will be used inappropriately.

17. The correct answer is C. This is the only statement that mentions the fears which people have about the procedure.

18. The correct answer is B. Paragraph 7 argues that "its detractors, like myself, insist that its defining feature is simply its larger size."

19. The correct answer is C. The idea that the project is a big one is the same thing as the idea that "its defining feature is simply its larger size."

20. The correct answer is A. The final paragraph presents the following argument: "Even if we can change our lifestyles, will we do so? Many people may treat susceptibility-prediction as inevitability, and relapse into even worse lifestyles."

21. The correct answer is C. Paragraphs 1 to 4 talk about "a new project [that] is underway to assist colleges that train students to teach vocational subjects."

22. The correct answer is B. This is the only answer choice that mentions the new project. The other statements are not directly related to this idea.

23. The correct answer is B. Paragraph 6 states that "results for ethnic minority children are rising faster than the average. Thus, what is needed is a far more plural system." "Plural" is synonymous with "diverse."

24. The correct answers are A and E. Paragraph 7 tells us that the system needs to "ensure that there is no devaluation of academic standards and college graduates have the skills required for a more competitive job market."

25. The correct answer is A. This is the only statement that focuses on academic standards and teachers' skills.

26. The correct answer is C. Paragraph 3 explains: "Governmental officials will suggest that some of the cash might be better directed to making buildings more environmentally sustainable . . . or boosting pre-school learning."

27. The correct answer is C. This is the only answer choice that indicates that there is a dispute about what the money should be spent on. The phrase "some of the cash might be better directed" indicates that there is disagreement on this issue. Answer D indicates that a dispute exists, but it does not explain the nature of the dispute.

28. The correct answer is B. Paragraph 9 states: "The report on the Building Schools for the Future (BSF) program . . . says the scheme must be regularly reviewed."

29. The correct answer is D. Paragraph 9 points out that local authorities have complained that "the government may force them into becoming private academies as part of BSF."

30. The correct answer is B. This is the only answer choice that mentions private academies.

31. The correct answer is D. The writer uses the phrase "small fiddle" to mean a false claim for what they believe to be an insignificant amount. You should know that "fiddle" means to tamper with, so this question shouldn't give you too much trouble, provided that you have read the answer choices carefully. Answer A is erroneous because it does not mention the idea that the claim must be fraudulent. Answers B and C are incorrect because they don't mention the idea that the policyholder him- or herself considers the amount to be insignificant.

32. The correct answer is C. The main idea of the article is stated in paragraph 1: "However, many people do not realize that the insurance industry has had to fight increasing insurance fraud." The author explains in paragraph 2 that most people are not only unaware of the amount of fraud, they also do not actually know what actions constitute fraud.

33. The correct answer is A. In the previous question, we have discovered that people do not know what constitutes fraud. The author supports the idea that most people do not understand what constitutes fraud by giving a definition of fraud: "Essentially fraud is committed any time a policyholder asserts that he or she has suffered a theft or other loss which was not actually suffered and is submitting a claim to the insurance company to receive reimbursement. "

34. The correct answer is A. The fifth paragraph states: "Perpetrators of insurance fraud also feel vindicated because of the knowledge that they have paid premiums for a certain number of years, so they believe that they deserve something back from the insurance company. The phrase "feel vindicated" is synonymous with the idea of justifying your behavior.

35. The correct answer is C. This is the only answer choice that mentions the idea of vindication or justification of the behavior.

36. The correct answer is D. The writer makes no claim about the propensity of the average household to participate in local recycling schemes. While you may be tempted to think that this answer choice is claimed in the text because of the writer's comment about dumping items on the side of the road, the writer is only talking about some odd occurrences of this behavior, not what the average household does.

37. The correct answer is C. We could always use outdated equipment or we could even decide not to use a computer at all. However, most people will want the newest equipment, so in this way, the computer industry causes the problem. Answers A and B are not stated or implied in the text. Answer D is a fact, not a claim.

38. The correct answer is B. The writer places the word "enforces" in quotation marks in this sentence to show that the word is not used in its literal sense. The purchase of new computers really isn't obligatory because it isn't actually enforced. The computer companies don't regulate or monitor computer purchases in the same way that police enforce laws, for example. Nor are we obliged to buy computers. However, as stated in the previous explanation, most people are going to want up-to-date equipment.

39. The correct answer is D. The statement that "Printers just need the ink or toner cartridges removed before dismantling them" does not provide a logical step in the structure of the writer's argument because up to this point in the text, the writer has been talking problems with the disposal of computer equipment. The disposal of printer cartridges isn't really a problem anymore, according to the text, because the disposal practices mentioned in this paragraph "have been around for quite a while now." This doesn't support the flow of the argument. It is merely extra information.

40. The correct answer is A. The main cause of environmental damage from computer disposal today is that toxic gases from computers that are not disposed of properly are being released into the earth and atmosphere. Remember to re-read the first and last paragraphs closely when responding to 'main idea' or "main cause" questions. The first paragraph states: "Because computers contain many parts that could release toxins into the soil, city governments are seeking alternative ways to dispose of antiquated computers, as well as all disused electronic equipment." Answer choice C is a specific detail from the article, and the other answer choices are not stated or implied in the text.

GRAMMAR AND USAGE EXERCISES – SET 1

1. C
2. B
3. A
4. C
5. D
6. A
7. B
8. A
9. C
10. A
11. C
12. B
13. D
14. C
15. B

GRAMMAR AND USAGE EXERCISES – SET 2

1. D
2. D
3. C
4. D
5. C
6. D
7. B
8. C
9. C
10. A

11. B

12. A

13. D

14. C

15. A

GRAMMAR AND USAGE EXERCISES – SET 3

1. A

2. C

3. A

4. B

5. A

6. A

7. C

8. B

9. C

10. A

11. A

12. D

13. B

14. B

15. B

GRAMMAR AND USAGE EXERCISES – SET 4

1. The correct answer is A. We need the noncomparative adjective "anywhere" because we are not making a comparison in the sentence.

2. The correct answer is B. We are indicating that the job is nearly done, so we need the adverb of degree "almost."

3. The correct answer is D. The emphatic form is needed here because we are contrasting the accident to the carefulness. The action is in the past, so the correct answer is "did have."

4. The correct answer is B. We need the accusative form "me" because of the preposition "between."

5. The correct answer is C. The plural form is required because of the plural noun "people" earlier in the sentence.

6. The correct answer is A. The relative pronoun "whose" is correct since the name belongs to the student.

7. The correct answer is B. We are describing a strong obligation or expectation in the recent past, so we need to use "should have" in this sentence.

8. The correct answer is A. We know that the superlative form is needed in this sentence because of the article "the."

9. The correct answer is D. The connective "in spite of that" is needed because of the word "but," which shows a contrast is going to be made. The other answer choices are not grammatically correct.

10. The correct answer is D. This is a form of the third conditional, so the inverted form of the past perfect "had I had" is the correct answer.

11. The correct answer is A. The verb "decide" takes the infinitive, so "to attend" is the correct answer. Notice that the verb "attend" in this context is a transitive verb, so we don't need a preposition.

12. The correct answer is C. "Get away with" means to escape the consequences of your actions.

13. The correct answer is B. The verb "be" is needed after the modal verb "can." We are describing an action, so we need the adverb "easily" rather than the adjective "easy."

14. The correct answer is C. "Not a word" is a negative adverbial clause, so we need to invert the auxiliary verb "did" to get the correct answer "did he say."

15. The correct answer is B. The word "all" needs the preposition "of." The definite article is needed because we are describing something specific, i.e., the new merchandise.

16. The correct answer is A. The passive form of the perfect infinitive is required since we have the verb "are believed."

17. The correct answer is B. The noun phrase "the beginning" needs to be preceded by the preposition "at."

18. The correct answer is A. We need the third conditional form in this sentence since we have the past perfect "hadn't eaten." Remember that you can use "might" instead of "would" in the third conditional.

19. The correct answer is B. We need the singular demonstrative pronoun "this" because the noun "book" is singular.

20. The correct answer is C. The need the plural form "others" because of the word "many."

GRAMMAR AND USAGE EXERCISES – SET 5

1. The correct answer is C. We have the negative adverbial "very rarely" so we need to invert the auxiliary verb for the correct form "does she appear."

2. The correct answer is A. The relative pronoun "that" is correct since there is a clause after the gap.

3. The correct answer is C. "Size up" is a phrasal verb that means to measure or estimate something.

4. The correct answer is A. The verb "hope" takes the infinitive form, so the correct answer is "to go." The perfect infinitive in answer choice D is incorrect because we are speaking about an action in the future.

5. The correct answer is C. "No sooner" is a negative adverbial, so we need to invert the auxiliary verb for the correct form "had we arrived."

6. The correct answer is D. The verb "recover" takes the preposition "from."

7. The correct answer is B. We have the third conditional here because of the verb "wouldn't have gotten." So, the past perfect "had she been" is needed in the second part of the sentence. We have not used the word "if," so we need to put the auxiliary verb "had" before the pronoun "she."

8. The correct answer is B. We can omit the use of a relative pronoun in this sentence. The correct word order is subject + verb + adverb, so we need the answer "I saw last week."

9. The correct answer is D. We need the bare form of the passive infinitive "be invited" because of the use of the verb "requested" and the relative pronoun "that."

10. The correct answer is C. The superlative form (without "the") is needed here because of the phrase "one of" earlier in the sentence.

11. The correct answer is A. We are talking about a strong obligation in the recent past, so the correct answer is "you should have filled."

12. The correct answer is B. We are making a comparison in this sentence to McDonald's, so we need the comparative adverb of place "somewhere else."

13. The correct answer is D. We need "most" because we are describing the majority of students.

14. The correct answer is A. The verb "deny" takes the gerund form, so "stealing" is the correct answer.

15. The correct answer is C. "Put up with" is a phrasal verb that means to tolerate something or someone.

16. The correct answer is B. We need the phrase linker "because of" since the gap is followed by a phrase, rather than a clause.

17. The correct answer is A. The word "other" is used to modify the plural noun "hobbies."

18. The correct answer is B. The emphatic form "do need" is correct since we are emphasizing a generalization or habit.

19. The correct answer is B. The active form of the perfect infinitive form "to have worked" is correct since the sentence is talking about an action in the recent past.

20. The correct answer is A. The pronouns "you and he" are needed he since they form the subject of this clause in the sentence.

SENTENCE FORMATION AND ESSAY DEVELOPMENT EXERCISES

1. The correct answer is B. The word "which" forms the beginning of a non-restrictive relative clause. This means that the clause beginning with "which" does not identify which tectonic plates we are describing, but provides extra information about the plates. Commas are needed after non-restrictive relative clauses.

2. The correct answer is C. The new clause elaborates on the cause of the increase in pressure. This concept is discussed in the next sentence of the essay: "Therefore, the two plates will eventually shift or separate since the pressure on them is constantly increasing." This new clause effectively elaborates on the topic of the paragraph and helps to maintain the flow of the essay.

3. The correct answer is B. Paragraph 1 describes the tectonic plates in the earth, as well as those at sea. Sentence 6 mentions that "tectonic plates cause earthquakes, both at land and at sea." So, to maintain the correct logical sequence, the best place for sentence 6 is after sentence 3.

4. The correct answer is D. The subject of the main clause of this sentence is "an occurrence." The word "occurrence" is singular, so the singular verb "is" must be used. We are describing a scientific fact, so the present tense is needed.

5. The correct answer is B. This is a question on the correct placement of modifiers. The action of the waves causes the destruction. The sentence as originally written suggests that the damage occurs only in the epicenter.

6. The correct answer is A. A question mark needs to go inside the final quotation mark when it is part of the original dialogue. In this essay, the dialogue consists of thoughts and questions within the speaker's mind.

7. The correct answer is C. Answer choice C is the best because it will make the essay more cohesive than the other options. The mention of "academic life" in the new clause provides a logical connection to the process of applying for college described in the main body of the essay. The mention of "something truly wonderful" connects to the outcome of receiving a scholarship, which the speaker mentions in the conclusion to the essay.

8. The correct answer is B. This is a question on parallelism. "Parallelism" means that you need to use the same parts of speech when you list items in a series. In this essay, we are listing two concepts, but "worry" is a noun and "doubting" is a verb. Answer B is the best because "worry" and "self-doubt" are both nouns.

9. The correct answer is D. "Self-recrimination and anxiety" are near synonyms to "self-doubt" and "worry" from the previous sentence, so these words would give the essay the best logical structure.

10. The correct answer is C. Answer choice C is more concise than the other choices. It also does not have an unnecessary comma like the other choices. No further comma is needed because this new part of the sentence does not use the word "I" again as a grammatical subject.

11. The correct answer is D. Lincoln was living in the house, so the house is the object in the clause. Therefore, we need to use the "in which" relative clause construction. This also helps us to avoid ending the sentence with a preposition.

12. The correct answer is A. The words "the notion" need to be immediately after the comma because these words refer back to "the idea" in the first part of the sentence. So, we can use a comma to join the new clause to sentence 6.

13. The correct answer is A. "In order to" is the best transition phrase because it describes the reason why Lincoln began to write to others. We use the phrase "in order to" to show cause and effect in this way in a sentence.

14. The correct answer is B. We are placing emphasis on Lincoln as a person, so we need to use the active voice. There are two verbs or actions in the sentence: garnering support and delivering speeches. The support occurred as a result of the speeches, so the speeches came first. We normally need to use the past perfect active tense (had delivered) for the action that occurred first. The past simple active (garnered) is used for the second action.

15. The correct answer is C. The focus of the entire essay is on Lincoln, not Seward. So, the additional information about Seward is not necessary.

16. The correct answer is C. The colon placement is correct since several items are listed in a series after it. Also remember to put a comma after each word in the series that is before the word "and."

17. The correct answer is C. The grammatical subject of the clause is "a human being," which is singular. So, "his or her future" should be used in order to have agreement between the pronoun and antecedent.

18. The correct answer is C. Here we have two complete sentences, the first beginning with "epistemology" and the second beginning with "it." A semicolon can be used between two complete sentences in this way. The use of the semicolon in this way avoids inappropriate run-on sentences.

19. The correct answer is A. The grammatical subject of this sentence is "human personality," which is singular. The present tense is needed since we are discussing facts and theories.

20. The correct answer is B. The topic sentence of this final paragraph focuses on the unity of the human being, so the mention of "unity or wholeness" in the new text provides support for the main idea of the paragraph.

21. The correct answer is D. The subject of the sentence is "cell division," which is singular. So, we need to use "it is" instead of "they are."

22. The correct answer is B. In this sentence, "affect" is used as a verb meaning resulting in, while "effect" is a noun meaning outcome.

23. The correct answer is D. The words "from cancer in the United States" form a phrase, not a clause. Therefore, no comma is needed.

24. The correct answer is A. You may be tempted to select answer choice C, but answer choice A is better for stylistic reasons as it correctly joins the clause to the sentence, while avoiding two words ending in "ing" together being placed together.

25. The correct answer is C. For better concision, the words "which would decrease the chance of getting cancer" should be deleted as they repeat the notion that "cancer risk can be reduced," which is mentioned at the start of the same sentence.

PUNCTUATION AND CAPITALIZATION REVIEW EXERCISES

1) B
2) C
3) D
4) B
5) A
6) A
7) D
8) C
9) E
10) B
11) A
12) B
13) B
14) A
15) E
16) A
17) A
18) C
19) A
20) E

SENTENCE CORRECTION AND REVISION PRACTICE SET 1

1. The correct answer is D. The phrase *Although only sixteen years old* modifies the pronoun "she." Therefore, "she" needs to come after this phrase.

2. The correct answer is A. This question is an example of the inverted sentence structure. When a sentence begins with a negative phrase [no sooner, not only, never, etc.], the present perfect tense [have + past participle] must be used. In addition, the auxiliary verb "have" must be placed in front of the grammatical subject of the sentence [I].

3. The correct answer is B. This question is about "parallelism." In order to follow the grammatical rules of parallelism, you must be sure that all of the items you give in a list are of the same part of speech. So, all of the items must be nouns or verbs, for example. In other words, you should not use both nouns and verbs in a list. Answer B has all nouns, but the other answer choices have some nouns and some verbs.

4. The correct answer is D. This question is about the use of punctuation. "However, the noise next door made it impossible" is a complete sentence. It has a grammatical subject [the noise] and a verb [made]. "However" must be preceded by a period, and the new sentence must begin with a capital letter. In addition, "however" is a sentence linker. So, "however" must be followed by a comma.

5. The correct answer is A. The words "which would be spacious enough to transport her equipment" form a restrictive modifier. A restrictive modifier is a clause or phrase that provides essential information about a noun in the sentence. In other words, we would not know exactly what kind of new car she wanted without the clause "which would be spacious enough to transport her equipment." Restrictive modifiers should not be preceded by a comma.

6. The correct answer is C. The prepositional phrase "Near a small river at the bottom of the canyon" describes the location of the people when they made their discovery. So, the prepositional phrase must be followed by "we." Since the prepositional phrase is at the beginning of the sentence, the complete phrase needs to be followed with a comma. Note that you need to put in only one comma at the end of such prepositional phrases.

7. The correct answer is B. This question tests your knowledge of "who" and "whom." Remember to use "who" when the person you are talking about is doing the action, but to use "whom" when the person is receiving an action. In this sentence, the candidate is receiving the action of being selected. So, the question should begin with "whom." The auxiliary verb "did" needs to come directly after "whom" to have the correct word order for this type of question.

8. The correct answer is A. The phrase "Always and Forever" is an example of a restrictive modifier. As mentioned in question number 5, restrictive modifiers are clauses or phrases that provide essential information in order to identify the subject. In other words, without the phrase "Always and Forever" in this sentence, we would not know exactly which song they played at their wedding. So, the phrase conveys essential information. Note that restrictive modifiers should not be preceded by a comma.

9. The correct answer is B. In this sentence, the word "as" functions as a subordinating conjunction. Commas should not be placed before subordinating conjunctions. Other examples of subordinating conjunctions are "because" and "since."

10. The correct answer is C. If you are talking about yourself in an imaginary situation, you need to use *were* instead of *was*. This is known as the subjunctive mood. In the other half of the sentence, you need to use the verb "would" when you are describing an imaginary situation.

SENTENCE CORRECTION AND REVISION PRACTICE SET 2

1. The correct answer is C. This question is about the use of punctuation. "However, they were out of reach" is a complete sentence. It has a grammatical subject [they] and a verb [were]. "However" must be preceded by a period, and the new sentence must begin with a capital letter. Compare the placement of "however" and the punctuation in these sentences: The child tried to grab the cookies from the shelf. They were, however, out of reach. When you use the word "however" in the middle of a sentence, "however" must be preceded by a comma and also followed by a comma.

2. The correct answer is C. "Covered in chocolate frosting" is a past participle phrase that describes the cake. In other words, the hostess is not covered in chocolate frosting. Therefore, the words "the cake" must follow the past participle phrase. Remember: past participle phrases are those that begin with verbs that end in -ed (in the case of regular verbs). You need to be sure that you have the participle phrase next to the noun that the phrase is describing.

3. The correct answer is A. This is another question about "parallelism." Be sure that all of the items you give in a list are of the same part of speech, nouns or verbs, for example. In other words, you should not use both nouns and verbs in a list. In addition, all of the verbs you use must be in the same tense. In answer A, both verbs are in the "to" form. The other answers combine -ing and -ed verbs.

4. The correct answer is A. The words "one which he could use to gaze at the stars" form a dependent relative clause. A relative clause often contains "that" or "which." A dependent clause cannot stand alone as a complete sentence. Since it is a non-restrictive (non-essential) relative clause, it must be preceded by a comma.

5. The correct answer is C. This question is another example of the inverted sentence structure. When a sentence begins with a negative phrase [no sooner, not only, never, etc.], the past perfect tense [had + past participle] must be used. In addition, the auxiliary verb "had" must be placed in front of the grammatical subject of the sentence [I].

6. The correct answer is B. This question tests your knowledge of conditional sentence structures. Conditional sentences often begin with the word *if*. Conditional sentences may express generalizations, as in this sentence. Therefore, the simple present tense (go) is used in the "If" clause, and the simple present (try) is also used in the main part of the sentence. The two parts of a conditional sentence must be separated by a comma.

7. The correct answer is B. Punctuation should be enclosed within the final quotation mark when giving dialogue. The word *said* shows that the comma needed.

8. The correct answer is D. The phrase "is known as" must be preceded with a noun phrase. "The experience of confusion about one's own identity" is a noun phrase. "Is known as" must not be preceded with a verb. No comma or pronoun (e.g., this, it) is needed.

9. The correct answer is C. "Upset from receiving the bad news" modifies or describes Mary. So, this phrase must be followed with a comma. No additional commas are needed.

10. The correct answer is D. "Dilapidated and disheveled" is a past participle phrase that describes the house. Therefore, "Dilapidated and disheveled" must be followed by a comma.

SENTENCE CORRECTION AND REVISION PRACTICE SET 3

1. You should select: No error. The sentence contains no errors in grammar or usage.

2. You should select: their. The antecedent is "chicory," which is singular. So, the pronoun "it" should be used before the grammatical subject, rather than "their."

3. You should select: compositions are. The grammatical subject of this clause is the word "what." Therefore, we need to use the singular form of the verb (is).

4. You should select: organ's. The plural form "organs" is needed. The possessive form "organ's" is incorrect because there is no corresponding noun for the possessive.

5. You should select: No error. The sentence contains no errors in grammar or usage.

6. You should select: to. The verb "differentiate" takes the preposition "from", not "to."

7. You should select: no. The sentence contains a double negative since the word "cannot" is used earlier in the sentence. So, "any" should be used here.

8. You should select: roman. Roman is a proper noun, so it needs to be capitalized.

9. You should select: among. Only two counties are mentioned, so the word "between" is needed.

10. You should select: the comma. The comma is incorrect since it unnaturally divides the subject and verb of the clause.

11. You should select: explorer's. The second part of the sentence is describing more than one explorer since the word "them" is used later in the sentence. Therefore, the plural possessive is needed (explorers').

12. You should select: die. The sentence is written in the past simple tense, so the verb form "died" should be used.

13. You should select: effected. The verb form (affected) is required since the sentence is talking about the changes that were a result of the Women's Rights Movement.

14. You should select: constitute. The subject of the sentence is "migration" so the singular verb form (constitutes) should be used.

15. You should select: and. We can see the use of "not only" earlier in the sentence, so we need "but also," instead of "and also"

16. You should select: that. The subject of this part of the sentence is the plural "settlers," so the plural pronoun "those" is needed, rather than "that."

17. You should select: having played. The perfect infinitive verb form "to have played" is needed because we are talking about a topic that has current relevance. We know that the topic is under current discussion because of the word "arguably" earlier in the sentence.

18. You should select: having. The subject of the sentence is "system," so the present simple verb form "has" is needed.

19. You should select: principle. You should use the word "principal" as an adjective in this sentence, rather than the noun form "principle."

20. The correct answer is C. The antecedent is "Siluriformes," which is plural. However, "its mouth" is singular. Therefore, the plural pronoun "their" and the plural noun "mouths" need to be used in order to correct the error.

21. The correct answer is C. Because of the placement of modifying phrase at the beginning, the sentence as written suggests that the tire is driving the car. The pronoun "I" needs to be placed after the introductory phrase since the speaker was driving the car. Remember to place the modifying phrase directly before the noun that it modifies.

22. The correct answer is B. The sentence contains a lack of parallel structure ("for having worked [. . .], retaining [. . .], and the special"). Answer B correctly uses the –ing form in all three verbs in order to correct the error.

23. The correct answer is D. The sentence as written is an example of a run-on sentence. The word "but" correctly subordinates the second part of the sentence.

24. The correct answer is E. The sentence has an error in parallelism. All of the hobbies should be stated in the –ing form, so E is the correct response.

25. The correct answer is D. This sentence also has an error in parallelism. All of actions should be stated in the –ed (past simple) form, so D is the correct response.

26. The correct answer is C. The sentence has an error in parallel construction, since it uses the –ed form of the verb ("disregarded") and the –ing form of the verb ("rebelling") in the same part of the sentence. There is no problem with the relative pronoun usage ("who") in the original sentence. Answer C correctly uses "who" and constructs both verbs in the –ed form

27. The correct answer is E. The sentence as written is a fragment. Replacing the –ing form "having" with the past simple tense ("avoided") completes the sentence correctly since the action described in the sentence occurred in the past.

28. The correct answer is C. The sentence as written incorrectly implies that the rocks, rather than the minerals, form the crystals. Response C corrects this error by using the verb "to form."

29. The correct answer is B. The highlighted part of the sentence is missing a relative pronoun ("that"). In addition, a comma needs to be placed before the grammatical subject of the sentence ("the congressman").

30. The correct answer is C. Since the pronoun "you" is used in the second part of the sentence, the same pronoun is also required in the first part of the sentence. The sentence is describing a generalization, so the present simple tense ("message") is needed, rather than the continuous form ("messaging").

SENTENCE CORRECTION AND REVISION PRACTICE SET 4

1. You should select: the comma. Remember that a comma should not be used before "that" when forming relative clauses.

2. You should select: themselves. The subject of this clause is "any substance," so the singular form of the pronoun (itself) should be used.

3. You should select: moorish. Moorish is a proper adjective, so it needs to be capitalized.

4. You should select: no error. The sentence contains no errors in grammar or usage.

5. You should select: spanned. The bridge spans the bay, so the passive verb form (is spanned) is needed in this sentence.

6. You should select: used. The sentence is describing a scientific principle, so the present simple tense (use) is required.

7. You should select: no comma. A comma should be placed after the adverb "theoretically" since this adverb is placed at the beginning of the sentence.

8. You should select: the semicolon. The word "however" forms a new sentence because it is capitalized, so a period needs to be used here, instead of the semicolon.

9. You should select: no error. The sentence contains no errors in grammar or usage.

10. You should select: it evaluates. The subject of the sentence is "disciplines," which is plural, so the clause should use the plural form "they evaluate."

11. You should select: no error. The sentence contains no errors in grammar or usage.

12. You should select: having been assassinated. The perfect passive infinitive verb form "to have been assassinated" is needed because the word "indisputably" earlier in the sentence shows that this topic is still of current interest.

13. You should select: with. The word "impact" takes the preposition "on."

14. You should select: going. The simple present form of the verb "go" needs to be used in this sentence in order to form a parallel structure with the simple present form of the verb "be" in the "not only" clause of the sentence.

15. You should select: that make. The subject of the clause is "sequence", which is singular, so the verb "makes" is needed.

16. You should select: no error. The sentence contains no errors in grammar or usage.

17. You should select: no comma. A comma is needed before the word "who" because this part of the sentence forms a non-defining relative clause. In other words, the name of the king is provided, so this part of the sentence just gives additional information.

18. You should select: his. The subject of the clause is "work," which is singular, so the pronoun "its" should be used.

19. You should select: Northeast. The adjective should not be capitalized since it is not a proper adjective.

20. correct answer is B. The subject of the sentence is "colleges," so the plural form of the pronoun ("their") needs to be used. The Antebellum Period is in the past, so the past simple tense ("included") is the correct verb form.

21. The correct answer is E. The base form of the verb "see" is used in the second part of the sentence, so the verb "to overcome" is needed in order to create the correct parallel structure between the verb forms.

22. The correct answer is E. The subject of the sentence is singular ("a country's commerce"). Accordingly, the singular pronoun ("its") is correct. In addition, the infinitive verb form ("to grow") is required since the preceding verb forms are in the infinitive form ("to export [. . .] to invest").

23. The correct answer is C. The sentence describes an action that was completed in the past, so the past simple form ("promoted") is correct.

24. The correct answer is D. The sentence as written has a misplaced modifying phrase and thereby suggests that the embassy contains the confidential information. The letter, rather than the embassy, contains the confidential information, so the modifying phrase ("containing confidential information") needs to be placed directly after the noun to which it relates ("the letter").

25. The correct answer is C. All of the verb forms need to be in the –ing form in order to create the correct parallel structure.

26. The correct answer is A. The sentence is correct as written since both verbs in the modifying phrase are in the –ing form ("drafting [. . .] and serving").

27. The correct answer is D. The sentence as written suggests that the plant is popular simply because it is indigenous to the northern hemisphere. By beginning the sentence with "since," the correct emphasis is placed on the climbing aspect of honeysuckle, which is what makes the plant popular in patios and gardens.

28. The correct answer is B. The introductory phrase "overworked and underpaid" describes the grammatical subject "many employees." Therefore, a comma needs to be used after the word "underpaid."

29. The correct answer is E. The phrase "With its sub-zero temperatures and frozen landscape" describes Siberia, so the word "Siberia" needs to be placed after the comma.

30. The correct answer is D. As written, the sentence contains a fragment ("When air rises and condenses into precipitation"). Answer D is the only response that corrects the fragment without improperly using the demonstrative pronoun "this."

COMBINING SENTENCES AND IDENTIFYING FRAGMENTS

1. The correct answer is D. A full sentence must have, at a minimum, a grammatical subject and a verb that describes the grammatical subject. Here we have the sentence: The restaurant closes at midnight. The grammatical subject is *the restaurant* and the verb is *closes*.

2. The correct answer is D. The sentence is: Off we go on another adventure! The grammatical subject is *we* and the verb is *go*. The sentence begins with the adverb *off* to heighten the exclamatory form.

3. The correct answer is C. The sentence is: He hopes to start this summer. The grammatical subject is *he* and the verb is *hopes*.

4. The correct answer is A. This sentence makes the most sense and also has the correct cause-and-effect relationship.

5. The correct answer is A. The sentence begins with the idea of the length of the training, so it provides the best contrast. It is also the best grammatically.

6. The correct answer is B. The sentence begins with the idea of the acrimonious relationships, so it provides the best contrast. It is also the best grammatically.

7. The correct answer is B. *Staying alert* is a gerund phrase which is used as the grammatical subject of this sentence.

8. The correct answer is A. The sentence is in the imperative voice since it gives a command. The pronoun *you* (for the person receiving the command) is understood from the context.

9. The correct answer is C. The grammatical subject is *vacationing* and the main verb is *can come*.

10. The correct answer is A. This is the only option that gives the clauses of the sentence in the correct order that states the cause-and-effect relationship.

11. The correct answer is C. This sentence places the correct emphasis on his dislike of alcohol and is also correct grammatically.

12. The correct answer is D. This is the only option that gives the clauses of the sentence in the correct order that states the cause-and-effect relationship.

13. The correct answer is B. The grammatical subject of this exclamation is *we* and the main verb is *go*. The adverb *away* is placed at the head of the sentence to give the proper emphasis to the exclamation.

14. The correct answer is A. The sentence has a compound grammatical subject: The old, the new, the borrowed, and the blue. The main verb is the word *are*.

15. The correct answer is C. The gerund *talking* is the grammatical subject and the main verb is *can lead*.

16. The correct answer is B. This sentence uses the word *certain* to show that prerequisites do apply to some classes. This idea is erroneously omitted in Sentence A. Sentences C and D are verbose and poorly constructed.

17. The correct answer is A. This sentence is the only one with the correct cause-and-effect construction.

18. The correct answer is A. Sentences B and D suggest an erroneous cause-and-effect relationship, while sentence C is too terse.

19. The correct answer is A. The grammatical subject of the sentence is *they* and the main verb is the word *are*.

20. The correct answer is B. *Being caring* is a gerund that forms the grammatical subject of the sentence, while the main verb is the word *is*.

21. The correct answer is B. *Reading and swimming* is a gerund phrase that forms the grammatical subject of the sentence, while the main verb is the word *are*.

22. The correct answer is D. This sentence shows the correct chronological sequence of events.

23. The correct answer is C. This is the only sentence that conveys the events in the correct order of cause and effect.

24. The correct answer is A. This sentence correctly sets up the contrast between giving a message of deterrence and granting the lenient sentence.

25. The correct answer is C. For questions asking you to combine two sentences, look to see whether there is a cause and effect relationship between the two sentences. In this question, the woman works so hard on her presentation because she needs to persuade the audience. Sentence C is the only sentence that expresses this cause and effect relationship correctly.

IDENTIFYING CORRECTLY-WRITTEN WORDS AND SENTENCES

1. The correct answer is D. This question is about correct parallel structure, also known as parallelism. In order to follow the grammatical rules of parallelism, you must be sure that all of the items you give in a series are of the same part of speech. So, all of the items must be nouns or verbs, for example. In other words, you should not use both nouns and verbs in a list. Where verbs are used, they should be in the same tense. In sentence D, the words "enjoyed," "relaxed," and "ate" are all verbs in the past tense. Sentence A incorrectly uses adjectives ("fun" and "exciting") and verbs ("gave"), while sentence B mixes the –ing and –ed verb forms. Sentence C mixes adjectives ("elegant" and "comfortable") with nouns ("staff members").

2. The correct answer is C. For questions on subject-verb agreement, you need to be sure to use a singular verb with a singular subject and a plural verb with a plural subject. While this sounds straightforward, complications can arise with certain words like "each," "every," "neither," and "either," all of which are in fact singular.

3. The correct answer is B. Restatement questions like this are asking you to find a word that can be used to restate a phrase from the original sentence. The idea "I didn't believe it" from the first sentence is best restated by the word "doubted" in answer choice B. Note that answer C is not the best answer because your skepticism is about passing the test, not about the test in general.

4. The correct answer is A. The word "speak" is a verb, so it needs to be used with the adverb "loudly." The other answer choices are not grammatically correct.

5. The correct answer is B. This question is asking you about pronoun-antecedent agreement. Pronouns are words like the following: he, she, it, they, and them. An antecedent is a phrase that precedes the pronoun in the sentence. Pronouns must agree with their antecedents, so use singular pronouns with singular antecedents and plural pronouns with plural antecedents. Be careful not to mix singular and plural forms. Sentence A is not correct because "group" is singular, while "their" is plural. Similarly, sentence C is not correct because "student" is singular, while "their" is plural. Sentence D is not correct because "friends" is plural, while "he or she" is singular.

6. The correct answer is C. This is another question on parallelism. Answer C is correct because "cookies" and "cake" are both nouns. The other sentences mix different forms. Note that in answer D, "my friend" is needed, rather than "friend."

7. The correct answer is A. You may see a question on the exam like this one, which provides you with a grammatically incorrect sentence and then asks you to find the grammatically correct revision. In our question, we need to change the subject of the sentence to "my mother" from the possessive form "My mother's car." In addition, it is best to avoid including parenthetical information in sentences, like "I crashed it last month" in our sentence. Sentences B and D are not correct because they state that the accident itself annoyed the mother, when her annoyance was actually caused by the money not being reimbursed. Sentence C is incorrect because the phrase "whose car I crashed last month" needs to be offset by commas.

8. The correct answer is D. This is another cause and effect question. Remember that for questions asking you to combine two sentences, look to see whether there is a cause and effect relationship between the two sentences. In this question, the teacher got the software because she wanted students to use the most up-to-date program. Sentences A and B state the opposite: that the teacher used the software because it was already available. Sentence C is in the passive voice and leaves out any mention of the teacher, so it is not the best answer.

9. The correct answer is B. Remember that when you have to restate a sentence concisely, you are looking for a word that can be used to replace a phrase in the original sentence. In our original sentence, the phrase "to get around having to do so" means that the company wanted to get around paying income tax. The word "evade" from sentence B is the most concise paraphrase of this idea.

10. The correct answer is C. This is a question on clear pronouns. For questions on clear pronouns, look at each sentence to see if there is any doubt about what the pronoun refers to. In sentence A, we do not know if the job is inspiring or if her attributes are inspiring. In sentence B, there is some doubt whether it is the parties or the students in the class that the speaker does not like. In sentence D, we do not know if the speaker missed the bus or the interview.

11. The correct answer is C. Here is another question on pronoun-antecedent agreement. Sentence A is not correct because "all" is plural, while "his or her" is singular. Sentence B is not correct because "either" is singular, while "are" is plural. Sentence D is also not correct because "group" is singular, while "have" is plural.

12. The correct answer is A. Sentence A is correct because it uses verbs, all of which are in the simple past tense (woke up, got out, and drank).

13. The correct answer is D. The word "infer" means to judge someone's attitude from their tone of voice or from what they state indirectly.

14. The correct answer is B. "Members" is plural, so the plural pronoun "they" is used correctly in the second part of the sentence.

15. The correct answer is D. This original sentence incorrectly uses "the client's claim" as the subject of the sentence, rather than "the client." Sentences B and C have also incorrectly used "the client's claim" as the grammatical subject. Sentence A is not the best answer because it is preferable to avoid the practice of placing information in parentheses within sentences.

16. The correct answer is D. The sentences are correct as written.

17. The correct answer is A. We need the present perfect tense *has decided* since we are describing a past action that is of current significance.

18. The correct answer is D. The sentence is correct as written.

19. The correct answer is A. The plans are definite, so we should use *will* instead of *would*. Remember to use *would* in hypothetical or uncertain situations.

20. The correct answer is A. The sentence is describing the time that something will take place, so *when* is needed rather than *which*.

WORD MEANING, RELATIONSHIPS, AND CONTEXT

1. The correct answer is C. In the original sentence, the word *ache* is a verb that means to hurt. Sentence C is the only answer choice that also uses the word *ache* as a verb.

2. The correct answer is B. In the original sentence, the word *comb* is used as a verb in its metaphorical sense, meaning to search meticulously. In the other answer choices, the word is used as a noun or as a verb in the literal sense.

3. The correct answer is C. In the original sentence, the word *fly* is used as a verb that refers to the literal action of being airborne. The word is used idiomatically or as a noun in the other sentences.

4. The correct answer is B. In both sentences, the word *iron* is used as a noun to refer to the metallic substance. Sentence A refers to a home appliance, while sentences C and D use *iron* as a verb.

5. The correct answer is B. The verb *milk* is used metaphorically to mean taking advantage of a situation. In sentences A and D, we are talking about the dairy drink, and in sentence C, *milk* is used literally as a verb.

6. The correct answer is B. The word *matter* is used in both sentences as a noun that refers to the topic under consideration. In sentence A, we use the word *matter* in its scientific sense. In sentence C, the word is used in a metaphorical sense, and in sentence D the word is used as a verb.

7. The correct answer is B. In both sentences, the word *trust* is used as a verb to mean placing faith in someone. Sentences A and C use the word as a noun, while sentence D uses the word as an adjective.

8. The correct answer is C. In both sentences, the word *present* is used as an adjective to describe the attendance of someone at an event. Sentence A uses the word as a noun, sentence B uses the word as a verb, and sentence D uses the word to describe time, not attendance.

9. The correct answer is D The word *report* is correctly used in both of these sentences as a verb. Sentences A and B use the word as a noun referring to a written or spoken text, while sentence C uses the word as a noun in a different sense to refer to a noise.

10. The correct answer is C. In both sentences, the word *trade* is used an as adjective to refer to international commerce. Sentence A uses the word as a verb, while sentences B and D use the word as a noun.

11. The correct answer is C. The word *scratch* in these sentences is used as a verb to refer to the action of using the fingernails to relieve the sensation of itching. The word is used as a noun in sentences A and D, while sentence C uses the word in its metaphorical sense.

12. The correct answer is A. In these sentences, the word *produce* is used as a noun to refer to fresh fruit and vegetables. The word is used as a verb in the other sentences.

13. The correct answer is C. Sentence A confuses the word "affect" with "effect," while sentence B confuses "principal" and "principle." Finally, sentence D confuses "allusion" with "illusion." "Elude" is used correctly in sentence C, but be careful not to confuse it with "allude."

14. The correct answer is D. This is another question on commonly-confused words. Sentence A confuses "bale" with "bail," while sentence B confuses "pour" with "pore." Pay special attention to sentence C since the confusion of "adverse" and "averse" occurs very frequently.

15. The correct answer is B. "Illicit" means illegal. Do not confuse "illicit" with the verb "elicit." Sentence A confuses "bazaar" and "bizarre." Sentence C confuses "complement" and "compliment," while sentence D confuses "envelop" and "envelope."

CITATION AND REFERENCING

1. The correct answer is D. For questions like this one that are asking you about appropriate citation techniques, remember that the title of the article needs to be stated at the beginning of the sentence or in parentheses at the end of the sentence. For this reason, answers A and B are incorrect. Also remember that the information needs to be in quotation marks where two or more exact words are being quoted from the article. Finally, the citation needs to reflect the information from the article correctly. Answer C does not include any reference to the ethical and moral considerations, so it is not a full paraphrase of what is stated in the article. For these reasons, Answer D is the best answer.

2. The correct answer is A. The indication of a volume and issue number ["125(3)"] indicates that a scholarly journal is being cited. The other entries use italics incorrectly.

3. The correct answer is B. Only the title of the book should be in italics.

4. The correct answer is C. The reading list will show other books and articles on the subject that you are researching, so you can use it to identify further sources that you can read on your subject.

5. The correct answer is D. We know that a book is being cited because the title is given in italics. In addition, a year is given, rather than a specific date, which identifies the source as a book.

WRITING SKILLS EXERCISES

1. The correct answer is B. We are going to talk about why the IQ test is being replaced, and sentences A and D talk about where the IQ test is still in use, so they would not be appropriate. Answer C is also not suitable since it is critical of the theory of MI, and we are going to talk about those who are in support of MI.

2. The correct answer is C. The new sentence states that "75% of the schools in our district are now using placement tests based upon the theory of multiple intelligences." So, this supports the claim in sentence 1 that MI is replacing IQ.

3. The correct answer is A. This clause of the sentence is referring back to verbal or linguistic intelligence, which is singular. So, the third person singular of the pronoun and verb (it includes) is needed here.

4. The correct answer is D. We are talking about famous sports personalities, which is plural, so we need the plural pronoun and verb (they are) at this point in the sentence.

5. The correct answer is D. Sentence 12 makes a claim about teaching and learning, so it should come after sentence 9, which mentions "types of learners."

6. The correct answer is D. The grammatical subject of this clause refers to the phrase "a Herculean task," which means a task that requires a huge amount of work. The phrase "a Herculean task" is a singular noun phrase, so we should use another singular noun phrase (the work) at the start of this clause.

7. The correct answer is C. The phase "rather than regional" is grammatically correct and provides the best contrast to the geographical region of the western United States.

8. The correct answer is B. The use of the word "national" links back to the idea of national importance in the previous sentence. No comma is needed here since we have a restrictive clause that defines the memorial.

9. The correct answer is D. Sentence 12 in the original essay is actually a sentence fragment, so a comma is needed to join this phrase to the main clause of the sentence.

10. The correct answer is C. Putting the cost of the project in today's money is a useful addition because it emphasizes, in real terms, now expensive the project was.

11. The correct answer is A. The sentence as it is written provides the best link to Sentence 2, which describes the study of molecules, minute chemical compounds that are studied under a microscope.

12. The correct answer is B. The phrase "emitted from the instrument" modifies the noun "electrons," which is the grammatical subject of the sentence. The grammatical subject of the sentence is plural, so the verb "pass" is needed.

13. The correct answer is C. The essay is describing the electron microscope. The reference to old-fashioned cameras is off topic at this point in the essay.

14. The correct answer is A. The present passive continuous mood of the verb (is being studied) is best here because we want to put the emphasis on the action performed by the microscope, rather than on the scientists.

15. The correct answers are A and C. These two sentences are a good conclusion because the first one mentions the two types of microscopes which have been discussed in the essay, and the second one concludes the essay by giving it a forward-looking aspect.

16. The correct answer is B. We are describing the features of the two types of music, so the origin of a particular word is not relevant were.

17. The correct answer is C. Sentence 3 talks about monophonic music, while sentence 4 talks about polyphonic music. Since sentence 7 compares the two types of music, it is best placed after sentence 4.

18. The correct answer is D. Sentence 11 repeats the same ideas that have already been mentioned in sentence 10. Sentence 11 is redundant and should therefore be deleted from the essay.

19. The correct answer is B. The colon is used when we are going to list the items described previously. The colon needs to be used here as the student is listing the composers' names.

20. The correct answers are B and D. These two sentences mention that there are different types of classical music, as mentioned in the essay. They do not erroneously introduce new ideas in the conclusion to the essay.

21. The correct answer is B. The grammatical subject of the sentence is "support and concern," which is plural as two things are mentioned. The past simple plural (was) therefore needs to be used here.

22. The correct answer is D. "Elude" means evade, so it is the correct answer since we are speaking about something that the writer is not able to achieve. "Illude" means to delude or deceive. "Allude" means to refer to something.

23. The correct answer is C. Paragraph 2 of the essay describes how the student felt in the second grade. In paragraph 3, he is describing grades 3, 4, and 5, so we need the extra information here for continuity in the essay.

24. The correct answer is A. The dash can be used like a colon, so it can be used when someone is going to be named or something is going to be listed. The student is naming the teacher in this sentence, so the use of the dash is correct.

25. The correct answer is C. This is a personal experience essay, so the essay focuses on the experience of the student writing the essay. Sentence 14 describes the experience of other students, so it is extraneous and should be deleted.

Made in the USA
Monee, IL
12 September 2023

42615336R00083